*"My newspapering activity started many years ago,
selling the Muskegon* Chronicle *on the streets of Muskegon,
Michigan, where I lived in the early years of my life."*

Elmer L. Andersen

# VIEWS

*from the Publisher's Desk*

*Editorials by*

## ELMER L. ANDERSEN
former Governor of Minnesota

## NODIN PRESS

MINNEAPOLIS

97-2068

ISBN 0-931714-73-7

Nodin Press, a division of Micawber's Inc.
525 North Third Street
Minneapolis, MN 55401

*Dedicated to Eleanor*
to recognize with honor and gratitude
65 years of life, love, family, and
shared business activity and public service

# Contents

## *Individuals Remembered*

## Personal Recollections

## Political Parties, Candidates, Campaigns, Elections And Endorsements

## Public Policy Issues
### Facing Minnesota, The Nation and the World

#### MINNESOTA

#### THE NATION

THE WORLD

## Reflections

# PREFACE

My newspapering activity started many years ago, selling the *Muskegon Chronicle* on the streets of Muskegon, Michigan, where I lived in the early years of my life. We bought the papers for two cents, sold them for three cents, but when there was special hot breaking news, there were "EXTRAS." And if the news was particularly interesting or encouraging, we would get tips of a nickel, dime, even a quarter, with some saying "Keep the change, buddy." The second most exciting occasion of that kind was Armistice Day 1918. The nickels, dimes, and even the quarters flowed pretty freely that day. No one has ever been able to guess what was the greater occasion than Armistice Day for tips. It occurred a few years later when Jack Dempsey knocked out Jess Willard.

My mother had a sister who was an elementary school teacher. Aunt Lillian had books at her home so it was always a special treat for me to go there. I particularly remember one set that was called "Journeys Through Bookland." There were ten or twelve volumes of excerpts from famous children's literature. I do believe that got me going on the idea of collecting books and having some of my own to read and reread. I have never recovered from the book collecting addiction.

Another important early influence was a friendship with LeRoy Olson. We shared an interest in nature and almost every Saturday would go on a nature hike. In the spring it took the form of a bird hike, keeping a list of the dates of first viewing of birds and being particularly excited when the warbler migration took place. Also, during the later spring and summer, we would gather specimens from Mona Lake and bring them home to observe. We loved the transformation of tadpoles into frogs. We each set up a balanced aquarium in an old washtub and marveled that we could create a living situation so that the plants in the aquarium were generating enough oxygen to take care of the needs of the living animals.

These nature studies led to a suggestion to the editor of the *Muskegon Chronicle*, Archie McCrea, that I could write bird articles for the paper if they would consider publishing them. When he read a few samples, he agreed and began to print them. The first two or three were without pay, but then he felt it was only fair that I be paid and gave me $1.50 per article which I thought was wonderful compensation, which it really was at that time

That led to working as a "stringer" for the newspaper at the high school and community college in Muskegon as well as being active in starting a publication for the new community college.

In writing I was drawn to the essay form as a delightful type of writing, personal and light hearted: I still remember the first time reading Charles Lamb's essay on a roast pig which I thought was fascinating. Also, the work of Agnes Repplier interested me. So, nature, reading, writing, publishing all had very early roots.

On finishing junior college in 1928, I came to Minnesota; continued work for E.H. Sheldon & Company; entered the University of Minnesota, where I was editor of the *Minnesota Business Review*; graduated in 1931; was married to Eleanor Johnson in 1932; and joined H.B. Fuller Company in 1934. While working at Fuller, I still had the dream of some day having a weekly community newspaper.

Leaving day to day activity at H.B. Fuller Company in 1974, it occurred to me that I maybe could fulfill that long held dream of a weekly newspaper. I began to cast about, and wound up at Princeton, Minnesota, where we bought two bitterly competing newspapers, the *Princeton Union* and the *Princeton Eagle*, combined them into the *Princeton Union-Eagle*, and formed Princeton Publishing Company.

The editorial side of publication has always piqued more of my interest than the commercial, though I certainly recognize the importance of the latter. Early on I wrote "The Publisher's Notebook" and then began to write editorials on various local issues. The aim never was to tell people what to think or what to do so much as to stimulate thinking so they would be more informed and participating actively as citizens. A part of the *Princeton Union-Eagle* activity was involvement in East Central Minnesota Publishers (ECM), a central printing plant with other publishers. We gradually had an opportunity to acquire the papers of the other publishers and the Central Printing Plant. In putting together the elements into one unified company, it wound up with the name ECM Publishers, Inc., which we currently use. The company has grown and prospered with a publication division, a printing division, a distribution division, and, for some time, an office products division. At the present time, there are in excess of 450 regular part-time and full-time employees. So it has grown considerably from being the early dream of a weekly news-paper. There are now ten newspaper publications.

One newspapering philosophy would hold the publication apart from the community as a non-participating observer, an investigational report, and a confrontational influence in the community. We have not subscribed to that philosophy. We believe the newspaper in a community should be an inherent part of its development and growth and aid the community in achieving the dreams of the people. It should be honest and forthright in its reporting of facts as it learns them but also look for the positive news rather than becoming overly occupied with negative reporting.

Editorial writing is a fascinating and stimulating pursuit. One's mind has to be constantly on the alert for ideas and information, and the time spent researching, writing, and rewriting editorials can be a very satisfying experience. At least it has been for me. Becoming computer literate and using the computer as a word processing agent has eased the composition chore greatly. Typing, correcting, and retyping used to be very burdensome, but a computer makes it easier.

I am indebted to Russell Fridley, long-time director of the Minnesota Historical Society, who led the way to making that organization one of the best of its kind in the country, and suggested that the editorials I was writing had more than passing merit and a selection might be put together in a book. I responded by asking if he would edit such an effort, he agreed, and the result is this publication. We hope that it will be of some interest to readers.

*August 8, 1997*

Elmer L. Andersen

ELMER L. ANDERSEN

## A NOTE FROM THE EDITOR

Among the goals Elmer L. Andersen set for himself early in his youth were three: (1) to own and operate a farm (2) to serve in the state legislature and (3) to publish a newspaper. He achieved all three in addition to being elected Minnesota's 30th governor in 1960 and leading a small glue company in St. Paul to becoming a diversified corporation that today numbers among the *Fortune* 500.

This book stems from his career as a newspaper publisher and journalist, dreamed about as a young man, and the last of the three goals to be attained at the age of 67 in 1976. Over the past two decades he has written some 2,000 editorials and, for 15 of those 20 years, an additional weekly column entitled "The Publisher's Notebook." The editorials and columns that appear in these pages reveal the man and his Jeffersonian reach of interests — nature, farming, government and politics, history, literature, the arts and people of all kinds and persuasions. In his own words, he is "in love with living," and that zest for learning and living each day to the fullest plus his fondness for the written word not surprisingly led him into the world of journalism. The human condition and the natural world are continual sources of fascination and inspiration for him. These editorials and columns, many in essay form, drawn from his weeklies, provide the vehicle and opportunity for the reader to share his enjoyment of examining issues, people and places informed by the fresh and original insights he brings to them as our global village verges toward the 21st century. "Some of Elmer's best writing," observes Jaime Becker of St. Paul, "takes place when he is developing an idea not yet prevalent and uses his editorial to develop the concept."

In putting together the pieces making up this book, priority has been given to his nature pieces, profiles of persons he has known and followed closely, a few adventures and reflections on issues ranging from local to global. 18 have been taken from "The Publisher's Notebook" (TPN), one from the *Mille Lacs County Times* and the remaining 108 are editorials from the *Princeton Union-Eagle*. Notes in italics, introducing major sections of the book and preceding a number of the selections are those of the editor and not of Elmer.

RUSSELL W. FRIDLEY

# Minnesota's Ever-Changing Seasons

*One cannot live in Minnesota without being keenly aware of the state's changing and variable seasons and the daily effect they have on each of us, physically and psychologically. The arrival of Spring, the subject of the first editorial, in the spirit of Walt Whitman and Emily Dickinson, for the author, is a metaphor for rebirth, renewal and immortality.*

# Sing Loud, Sing Clear, Spring Is Here

### 3-4-93

When it's March in Minnesota, Spring has come, at least in our hearts. The days are longer, the sun is higher and warmer. There may be blustery snowfalls but we know that the glorious rebirth of nature is soon at hand. Birds know. They return from southern climes, sing courtship songs, brighten the landscape and busy themselves with nest building. Researchers still seek to identify the mysterious stimulus that starts their trek back and their nesting instincts but come March in Minnesota birds are busy.

There is another beauty of the time. Young people of the state come together to compare their skills in athletic contests to determine the state's best. But it's not only in athletics. There are state conferences of debaters, play performers, music and art producers. It is a time of accomplishment joy and parent, teacher and coach pride.

While humans cheer skill and accomplishment, nature stirs. Who cannot marvel at a swelling bud—the reawakening of life that has been dormant through severe weather. It is amazing that the tiny nucleus of life survives the frigid winds of winter and grows as temperatures warm. Spring green is that delightful color as buds open and release leaves. Spring flowers soon emerge rapidly and bloom spectacularly.

And what of that marvelous chrysalis, formed in the fall, as a caterpillar spun a wrapper around itself with a strong attachment to a limb of a shrub or tree then became transformed into the pupa of a butterfly that would free itself and come forth when Spring gives the signal. Spring! What a joyful time, what a series of miracles, what a life experience!

# Oh What A Beautiful Summer!

7-28-94

August is yet to come, but, so far, surely, this has been the most wonderful summer in memory. Rains have been timely and sufficient to keep the landscape green and lush. Lakes and ponds are at fine levels, How recently and how long drought plagued us and drained our lakes! Temperatures have been ideal, rarely exceeding 90. For the most part, farmers' crops are doing very well. Cornfields never looked better. A drive through the countryside on the back roads is a thrill. Frequent as rainfalls have been, they have come at night or early morning, only rarely interfering with outdoor activity. Even the birds seem more plentiful and tuneful. Areas that have missed bluebirds report they are coming back.

Each shrub, flower tree or plant is a miracle of nature. Every morning we pause to admire a particularly handsome oak in a neighbor's yard. What a marvel of science is its capillary action that can draw the water and nutrients from the depth of the soil, convert it to chlorophyll and convey it to the furthermost leaf. There another marvel, chlorophyll, the only substance that can do so, traps and uses the energy of the sun to generate this year's growth and next year's bud. As fall's cooler days come, nature withdraws the life giving sap, leaves provide a spectacular color display as they dry and die. Sap is stored in the roots, the tree stands as a mighty symbol through the cold and storms of winter ready to respond when spring comes again.

Minnesota's distinct and decisive theater of seasons is truly an experience most of us would miss by living in a "one season" climate where plant changes are much less noticeable. And of all years, *1994* must be remembered as special. Lawns have never looked more beautiful. Roadsides are green and loaded with daisies, asters, lilies, and other flowers of the season. Ducks and geese are on the lakes, deer browse casually along highway shoulders, birds flit from shrub to shrub feasting on the bountiful fruit. This is a time to hike, bike, drive, run, camp, picnic, canoe, golf, fish, swim, sun, play and make the most of all the pursuits so available for family enjoyment. Enjoy, enjoy, enjoy!

🌲🌲🌲🌲

# Once Again Autumn Coloring Brightens Our Landscape

### 9-30-93

For many, autumn is Minnesota's most beautiful season. Last Saturday fall coloring was not at its height on the North Shore but far enough along, and so brightened by brilliant sunlight, to be stunningly beautiful. Nature's seasonal cycle is a miracle.

Chlorophyll is the magical substance in plants that converts the sun's energy into growth. It generates the green leaves of springtime. As the days grow shorter the green chlorophyll becomes less dominant and reds and yellows come to the fore. There are many colors of chlorophyll and individual characteristics of plants and trees. As the green recedes the other colors take over. From what we learn it is a matter of seasonal change and light rather than cold or frost.

Cold is a factor in "hardening off" trees for the dormant season. If severe cold comes before conifer sap has retreated to the root structure, cells can be ruptured, needles die, and can damage if not kill the tree. As sap leaves the upper parts of the tree desiccation ends the colorful season and the leaves turn brown or wither and die. Their contribution continues as they fall to the forest floor to nurture the host tree or other plants and seedlings.

While all this is going on the buds for next years growth are maturing and pushing off the base of the leaf stems causing leaves to drop. Some oaks can keep leaves all winter. Only when the buds begin to swell in the Spring do the leaves finally fall.

One of the delights for children of an earlier time was the frost that would form on single pane windows during the late fall and winter. Jack Frost was that delightful sprite who flitted about at night sketching fantastic designs. We also credited him with including his paint brushes and colors with him to touch up the leaves.

Observing and enjoying the marvels of nature is absorbing, relaxing and puts everything else in perspective. As a troubled William Cullen Bryant once wrote as he observed a waterfowl flying at dusk:

> *He who from zone to zone*
> *Guides through the boundless sky thy certain flight*
> *In the long way that I must tread alone*
> *Will lead my steps aright.*

# Mother Nature Gets Ready For Winter

### 10-29-92

To speak of Minnesota as a theater of seasons is an appropriate metaphor for the curtain does seem to rise and fall as we move from one act to another of each year's performance. Sometimes it is not as orderly and consistent as it might be, and at times a change can come abruptly as it did last Halloween. Most of the time, as this year, the pace is more leisurely and the transition provides marvelous days of mild temperature and scenic beauty as Mother Nature goes about the work of preparing for winter.

If one seeks peace and serenity and an escape from the hassle of urban life, one reassuring experience is a walk in the woods. As leaves have been pushed from their nodes by the formation of next year's buds, there is at once the ending of one life and the evidence of a life to come. Life is a continuum. Maybe it is because there are not leaves to give wind its sound, but a calm seems to settle over the landscape. There is a stillness as birds have departed and one only hears the occasional protest of crows or the urgent call of late departing geese.

A richly colored sunset over a still lake on the edge of the woods is a quiet drama of depth and power. One feels scales of harassment fall away and a resurging of calm confidence. Deep within us we feel a unity with the earth, the trees, the water as if we are returning to a long ago close association. As night falls and the earliest stars appear the immensity of our universe comes home to us, our relative insignificance, and the triviality of whatever had been a concern. It is as if we were carried away in a dream and lost in the wonder of it all.

Any seasonal transition has its appeal but there is a special character to Mother Nature's preparation for winter that can be a personal experience of a spiritual quality not to be missed. It is so available in Minnesota. It is so exceptional in Minnesota. We should never stray too far from communing with nature, nor for too long.

🌲🌳🌳🌲

## The Beauty Of That First Snowfall
11-26-87

It comes softly and quietly, frequently at night. It's pristine whiteness gives a fresh appearance to our yards and fields: we stop to admire. Suddenly we are aware that tree branches are in clear relief. As each twig has grown to give its leaves maximum sunlight a balanced pattern is produced. Now, with the leaves gone, the silhouette is remindful of delicate Japanese etched art.

There is a beauty that comes with that first snowfall that is unique to its season. Nothing else quite compares with it. It is emotional. Dirt, death and neglect are all covered over and that white blanket brings a sense of forgiveness, rest, and peace. The growing seasons have died but a sense of the promise of new life that is to come is part of the quietness. The eternity of nature, the wonder of death that is a condition of a new life, leads one's mind to philosophical musings.

To stand for a few minutes and surrender to the spell of another season, what it is, what it means—is to enjoy and draw much from the contemplation of that first snowfall.

# Holidays, Special Days, Anniversaries

*Special days, such as holidays and anniversaries, provide an editorial writer, as well as anyone, with a convenient peg on which to enlarge and deepen one's perspective in reviewing any subject over a span of time.*

# Leap Year Brings Thoughts Of Calendars

12-28-95

Our calendar does not perfectly mark the passing of a year so every four years we add a day to use up the time that has been accumulating. That fourth year has been called leap year and also included the quaint idea that women could propose marriage to the object of their affection without doing violence to appropriate modesty in such matters. Calendars have intrigued scientists, political and even church leaders for thousands of years. They were usually based on natural phenomena such as the cycle of the sun through the seasons or the phases of the moon. A problem developed as measurements became more precise. The solar year is 365 days, 5 hours, 48 minutes and 46 seconds. The lunar year (12 synodic months of 29.53 days) is 354 days, 8 hours, 48 minutes. People have used arbitrary devices to accommodate the difference. Ours is the Gregorian calendar, most widely used, which evolved from an action of Julius Caesar in 40 B.C. to clear up confusion. It established the Julian calendar which survived, despite some defects, until the 16th century when Pope Gregory XIII ordained the dropping of some days to get the equinox back to March 21 and established the Gregorian calendar its version of the leap year arrangement. The non-Catholic countries did not at first accept the new calendar. It was not until 1732 that England came along and the 20th century before the Eastern Church made the change. The church year, with long established Holy Days, stimulated the church's involvement. One of the important considerations was the belief that Jesus's resurrection occurred on Sunday. The Council of Nicea worked out the plan that perpetuates Easter on Sunday but not necessarily the same date each year. An interesting development was the Aztec calendar, one of the most accurate and the Muslim calendar with a lunar base. The history of calendars is fascinating, can be extensive and is not as arcane as might appear. As world communication has become instantaneous, calendar uniformity will gradually come, as will a uniform system of weights and Measures where America is the holdout. Maybe even a universal language will be agreed on.

🌲🌲🌲🌲

## Lincoln's Challenge Is For All Generations

2-10-94

It was in the midst of a dreadful war between the states—a war that divided families, that had turned the north and south against each other. A weary nation and an exhausted president paused to dedicate a cemetery. It had been established to provide for the heavy losses at the battle of Gettysburg—a battle that hit Minnesota hard. The first Minnesota regiment suffered a higher percentage of loss than any military unit in the history of the country.

President Abraham Lincoln made the sad journey from Washington to Gettysburg by train, scratching out, on the way, in sorrow but steadfast purpose, some appropriate remarks. Edward Everett, leading orator of the time, gave a long and eloquent speech, which no one remembers. Lincoln's words have come to be regarded as one of the most magnificent statements in the English language. It should be continually inscribed on the consciousness of Americans of every generation. Here is what he said:

12

*"Four score and seven years ago our fathers brought forth upon this continent a new nation, conceived in liberty, and dedicated to the proposition that all men are created equal. Now we are engaged in a great civil war, testing whether that nation, or any nation so conceived, and so dedicated, can long endure. We are met on a great battlefield of that war. We have come to dedicate a portion of that field as a final resting-place for those who here gave their lives that that nation might live. It is altogether fitting and proper that we should do this. But in a larger sense we cannot dedicate, we cannot consecrate, we cannot hallow this ground. The brave men, living and dead, who struggled here, have consecrated it far above our poor power to add or detract. The world will little note, nor long remember what we say here, but it can never forget what they did here. It is for us, the living, to be dedicated here to the unfinished work which they, who fought here, have thus far so nobly advanced. It is rather for us to be here dedicated to the great task remaining before us, that from these honored dead we take increased devotion for that cause to which they gave the last full measure of devotion; that we here highly resolve that these dead shall not have died in vain; that this nation, under God, shall have a new birth of freedom, and this nation of the people, by the people and for the people shall not perish from the earth."*

# Easter Is A Joyful Time For All

### 4-13-95

For adherents of the Christian faith Easter is one of the profound religious observances—marking the resurrection of Jesus Christ following his crucifixion and death three days earlier. It is the celebration of Christ's power over death and brings salvation and hope of life after death to all Christians. Easter marks the end of the penitential period of Lent.

The word Easter comes from an old English word Eastre, the name of a pagan spring goddess. Easter has become secularized and now has several identifications. It is associated with children. Egg hunts, the coloring of eggs in fancy patterns, the preparation and giving of Easter baskets containing candy and other treats are all part of the childrens' celebration.

It has become a time for parades of bands and floats, but also of fancily dressed citizens parading down Fifth Avenue. It is the casting off of winter blues and solemn hues and emerging in brightly colored spring costumes. Emerging butterflies are symbols of the metamorphosis. In our clime it marks the beginning of spring. We know that, although it may be a chilly and snowy day on Sunday April 9, Easter Sunday will be warmer and suddenly all the wonders of nature's spring will rush in upon us. within the following weeks hepatica, violets, bloodroot, marsh marigold, will appear and be the prelude for trillium, mocassin flowers and a host of other spring delights.

Gardeners know that the middle of April is vegetable planting time, especially if one is to have early June peas, the best of Bibb lettuce, and early brussel sprouts, cauliflower and other hardy varieties. Farmers watch the fields for the signs that the ground is ready for preparation and planting. Oak leaves that have clung tenaciously throughout the winter are now falling as swelling buds cast them off. Birds are quieter as they are busy building nests and laying their clutches of eggs. Fishermen and women eagerly prepare for their first spring outing.

All life is stirring, growing and blooming with vigor and vitality. As is so often declared, the distinctness of seasons gives Minnesota a special appeal. The Easter season brings together the deep faith of the religious, with the outpouring of Nature's beauty, and the anticipation of another season in a crescendo of uplift and joy. It is a glorious time!

🌲🌳🌲

*This national holiday, originally called "Decoration Day" has been formally observed since 1868 when Union General John A. Logan, Commander of the Grand Army of the Republic, called on members of the order to decorate soldiers' graves with flowers on the 30th of May.*

## Memorial Day Dedication

### 5-24-92

Monday is Memorial Day—a time for remembering. It is called Decoration Day by some, an occasion for decorating the graves—particularly of those who lost their lives in battle. This has made it a day of worship services and prayers for peace. It started in the Civil War years and has continued ever since.

This year the emphasis on peace may not be directed in people's thoughts to freedom from conflict with other nations but rather at how to avoid conflict among our own people here at home. It is worrisome to read of more and more people buying guns for self protection.

There is no question that we have developed a large underclass of deprived, uneducated, desperate and neglected children and young people for whom more must be done so they can enjoy mainstream lives of self respect and self support. We also simply must narrow the growing gap between the rich and the poor and strengthen the broad middle class that has been the mainspring of our prosperity in the past. Fortunately some programs are developing that encourage self sufficiency rather than permanent dependency.

Public officials must be candid in outlining how we reduce such programs as defense and foreign aid to accomplish the adjustments needed or face the need of increased revenues, and tell the people frankly. Voters should remove those who are part of the impasse, dealing in the double talk that we can have everything, reduce taxes and balance the budget. The reality may be harsh but it is time to face it.

The genius of our country is in the process that provides for balance between the branches of government and power in the people for orderly change. Greed, corruption, and the power of special interests have generated distrust by the people and the process of orderly change is threatened. The solution will not be in punishment and incarceration for protesters but a recognition of real problems and a determination to generate correction.

On this Memorial Day it is well to recall with thanks all that has gone before—but that is not enough this year—there must be the most serious dedication and personal commitment to make whatever sacrifice is needed to restore our nation to sensitive concern for the needs of the disadvantaged, to reestablish sound public finances, and return governmental service to public service dedicated to realizing the potential that our country can enjoy.

## There Is No Adequate Tribute

### 6-2-94

In addition to honoring all who have fought and died in our nation's military service, this year we are observing the 50th Anniversary of the storming of the Normandy Beaches in 1944, a successful operation that led to victory in World War II.

There are no words adequate to pay tribute to the devotion of the thousands who knew full well the price they could be required to pay yet rode the rough seas in landing crafts, braved a hail of fire, and fought their way through to break the lines of enemy defense. It cost a horrible price in lost lives. At the same time paratroopers were dropping behind the enemy line in another life threatening assignment. Overhead planes were breaching antiaircraft fire to destroy bridges and rail lines to hamper enemy troop movement. It has been described as the largest military operation in our history, in total numbers of ships, planes, troops and equipment. To travel across 70 miles of rough sea and deposit the assembled forces was an incredible task. The most important factor was the courage, confidence, and determination of the men to accomplish their mission.

One can still grieve for the thousands upon thousands of fine young men who gave their lives, and for the shattered families back home, the many young wives who had their dreams of love and family destroyed. One would think we had suffered enough through war to demand of our leaders that they bring about world peace under law that would end such carnage.

With the world now so closely knit, with all peoples everywhere having so much at stake, surely there must be a way to reach understanding. Unbridled ambition for power must be squelched and ruthless oppression and attack on people must be ended. We have done better at winning wars than projecting peace. If there is one message victims of war horror would send, if they could, it would be, "Don't let it happen again." If we applied the same resources and commitment to peace as we have done war, we could keep the faith with those who gave their all.

## Standing Up For America

### 6-28-94

When you read this you will probably have had your Fourth of July weekend. I hope you had a good time and made full use of that extra day. Also, the 4th is an appropriate time to think how lucky we are to be living in the United States of America, and at this particular time.

In earlier days times were tougher. In the pioneer days everyone had to work from dawn till dusk to clear land and survive. One hundred years ago many of the appliances, inventions, and conveniences that we take for granted had not yet been invented. Even in my own life time I have seen many changes. Seventy years ago I was in school but working nights, weekends and vacations in a school furniture factory. During the summer I worked 54 hours a week at 25 cents an hour. There were no deducts—but neither were there any benefits. There WAS no social security, no health insurance, no nothing. But I was very proud to bring home that check for $13.50 a week

Of more importance than the material benefits available to us today are the liberties we enjoy. Freedom to speak, to think, to differ, to travel, to work where we wish, to enjoy our families and homes. These are such important privileges—which many people of the world are still struggling to achieve. There is a requirement of us, if all that we enjoy in our country is to be retained. That is to respect the rights of everyone else, to respect those rights to worship as they chose, live their lives as they wish, so long as they let others do the same. Our country is becoming more and more diverse and with people more different from one another than was true in earlier immigration. One religion which was far away and unknown, Islam, is now the fastest growing religion in our country. We need tolerance and understanding to remain a peaceful society, particularly where matters of religion are concerned.

Not everyone has done equally well under our system of free enterprise and we need to help those who fall behind. The future peace and welfare of our country will not depend so much on what the government does but what we as individuals think and do. This election year is a test of the electorate to make sure we do not elect people who will work against the best interest of the country or who may not be qualified for the positions they seek. We must judge candidates by their actions and accomplishments and service not so much by what they say. Has their background been in public service? Have they served an apprenticeship in lesser positions before seeking a top position? Will they contribute to peace in our land or are they connected with organizations and activities that generate conflict and confrontation? If people give elections and candidates attention and study and make careful choices we will come out all right.

🌲🌳🌳🌲

## Hallowe'en Goes Back A Long Way

10-27-88

Be ready with treats Saturday evening as we celebrate Hallowe'en and children come to your door bedecked in outrageous costumes. Hallowe'en goes back a long way—to the sixth and seventh centuries—and derived from a combination of Druid and Christian celebrations. But today it is a time when witches and goblins abound doing all sorts of mischief if not appeased. We know about witches. They're the toothless, ugly old women in flowing black outfits and floppy hats that ride around on broom sticks to cast spells on the unwary. But what about goblins, what are they?

Our dictionary says that a goblin is "a grotesque sprite or elf that is mischievous or malicious toward people." Synonymous with goblins are gnomes and gremlins. Gnomes are small beings like little ugly old men, who live in the earth guarding mines, treasures etc. They terrify human beings by causing dreadful mishaps to occur. Gremlins are "invisible beings who were said by pilots in World War II to cause things to go wrong with airplanes." Editors know about gremlins for they creep into the printing plants at night and slyly slip things around to cause the typographic errors and misspellings that are the bane of the editor's existence, and not only once a year.

So be kind and generous to the creatures that call on Saturday evening and encourage them to mend their ways. And be sure to set your clock back one hour, before you go to bed.

🌲🌳🌳🌲

*Originally called Armistice Day because of its marking the end of World War I, it was changed to Veterans Day after World War II and dedicated to the American veterans of all wars.*

## Recollections Of Armistice Day

11-6-86

As a young boy I sold newspapers on the street in Muskegon, Michigan. Armistice Day, 1918 is memorable to me because it was one of the best days I ever had, selling "extras".

At that time newspapers were virtually the only source of news. When a special event occurred, there was an "extra"—a special edition with big headlines on the front page, the main story written special but most everything else from the previous edition.

Papers regularly sold for three cents. We paid two cents so had a penny profit. To sell 25 papers was a fair task after school. Sometimes in urging the sale of the last papers on prospects we would say "I've only two left" or whatever the case might be. We hated not to sell every paper because the loss cut deeply into those hard earned pennies. But when an extra came out, it was different. Papers sold like "hot cakes"—everyone wanted to get the big story. People would not wait for change. They would give a nickel, dime or even occasionally a quarter and say "keep the change" as they began to devour the news.

Armistice Day 1918 was a hysterically happy occasion. I was nine years old and impressed with the happy abandon with which people greeted the news—that on the 11th hour, of the 11th day of the 11th month fighting had ceased and the war to save the world for democracy was over.

How different everything was then. America's participation, for many, was a time of patriotic fervor. Troops went to Europe to the tunes of optimistic songs—"Over There," "K-K-K-Katy," "Margie," "Tipperary." There was tragedy and sadness when the casualties were reported, of course, but even that was often accepted with a kind of pride. Mothers who lost a son became Gold Star Mothers and many a window had the gold star banner prominently displayed for the passerby to see.

There was little doubting that the cause was worthy, that we had no choice but to enter when our shipping suffered attack. When it was over there was an enormous ticker tape parade when the troops began to arrive in New York and every community held parades and special programs to honor the returning soldiers.

How different the end of the Vietnam War. No victory, no pride of participation, no honor for the returnees. Finally, however, with the memorial in Washington listing those who sacrificed their lives, Vietnam veterans begin to feel they were appreciated, they are not now forgotten and their service is honored.

What of the future? Can war be avoided? Despite the many organizations and almost universal desire for peace our actions are similar to those which historically have led to war. We are investing heavily in armaments. As a nation we are not working as hard as is necessary for the institutions devoted to peace to become effective. Specifically, we have tended to give up on the United Nations instead of working to restructure it into a more representative body that we could trust.

As a national policy we pursue a singular course even to the concern of our traditional allies who find it hard to join with us when there is so little consulting prior to our policy decisions and actions.

Young people today tend to be fatalistic—yes, there will be another war, and if it is a nuclear holocaust there is a question whether civilization as we know it will survive.

Certainly the mood is a far cry from that of the first world war and armistice. We must take heart that history teaches that the worst scenarios somehow are avoided—the world does carry on—but today, nothing can be taken for granted. This Armistice Day can be a time of thanks that we have so far survived as a nation, that we have not had to endure a war within our own borders, and we can be profoundly grateful to those who, when called to serve, responded. Efforts for peace should command a high priority.

# Public Thanksgiving and Prayer

## 11-23-89

Thanksgiving was the first national holiday to be established by presidential proclamation. Both houses of Congress, in 1789, through a joint committee, sent a message to President George Washington, "requesting him to recommend a day of public thanksgiving and prayer to be observed by acknowledging with thankful hearts the many and signal favors of Almighty God, especially by affording them an opportunity to peaceably establish a form of government for their safety and happiness." President Washington responded with a proclamation issued October 3, 1789 setting Nov. 26th as Thanksgiving Day.

That presidential proclamation was exactly 200 years ago this year. But our minds and thoughts go back to the very first Thanksgiving in the fall following the landing of the pilgrims. In spite of all the hardships endured in their crossing, the fearsome struggle to get established, the decimating of their numbers by illness and accident, yet there was no question in the minds of those hearty pioneers that harvest time meant Thanksgiving.

We have had a recent reminder of how highly some people value what we too easily take for granted. Think of the struggle people went through to get out of East Germany and by a circuitous route go to West Germany and freedom. And then the exultation at the opening of the Berlin wall. Surely that reminds us how thankful, prayerfully thankful, we can be for the freedoms and opportunities we enjoy. There have been hardships for many this year, but even they will bow their heads in thanks come Thanksgiving Day that they were spared and that damages and losses were no worse. A spirit of thankfulness is a wonderful way to begin every day.

*Of the dates engraved on the memory of anyone alive at the time is the Japanese attack on Pearl Harbor. One is likely to remember where one was and the time of day when this stunning news was received.*

# Remembering Dec. 7, 1941

### 12-7-88

No December 7 can pass without recollections of that Sunday when its peace was broken by the sudden terse announcement over radio that the Japanese had bombarded Pearl Harbor. It was immediately evident that we were now in the war that we had been watching from afar. Germany had had so many successes in over running Europe that it seemed inevitable that we would be drawn in.

History may remember the end of the war with more emphasis than the beginning because of the first use of the nuclear bombs. In last Sunday's *New York Times Magazine* was the announcement that some manuscripts for President Harry Truman's second book are being shepherded to publication by his daughter and one chapter will tell of his most difficult decision, which was, of course, the bombing of Japan.

It was no sudden decision but brought about by our experts' appraisal of the lives that would be lost by a conventional invasion of Japan to win the war. Japanese fighters had a religious fanaticism—rather die than be defeated and were quite willing to fly kamikaze planes to certain destruction. Our people felt that would be magnified as they fought to protect their own country.

It was an agonizing decision for Truman but once made he felt it was the only thing to do, to quickly end the war and save hundreds of thousands of U.S. injuries and deaths. Now it is nearly fifty years ago but as freshly in mind as yesterday.

# 'So Hallow'd And Gracious Is The Time'

### 12-21-95

Belief in Christmas is very specific to Christians. It marks the birth of Jesus Christ, who came to save people from their sins, died on the cross, arose from the dead, returned to heaven to the right hand of God the Father and will return some day to gather the believers to be with Him forever. It is a profound commitment to faith and hope. Many believe that the return of Christ is imminent, will occur during the lifetime of people now living. For Christian believers Christmas is a joyful time of music, worship and celebration.

In addition to its specific religious significance to some among us, it has become generic, representing all that is best in the human spirit. Elements of the Christian story, such as the bringing of gifts, have become universal parts of what is termed the holiday season, or Holy Day season. Jewish people and other groups have religious observances at the same time. Traditions of our Christmas have come from many sources, some with pagan roots. Some think of all of this as a commercialization of Christmas, and, indeed, there are some excesses, but on the whole it is a wonderful time for all people everywhere, of whatever faith, or with none at all.

Christmas brings families and friends together in expressions of remembrance, love and appreciation. Christmas letters provide updates on family news and activities with warm good wishes for the season and the New Year ahead. Musicians have been inspired to produce songs and instrumental music of great beauty and emotional impact. Festivals of musical celebration are a highlight. All in all, the Christmas season is a revelation and demonstration of the universal love of people, far and near, known and unknown. Toys are donated so underprivileged children will have their gifts; food baskets are delivered; contributions fill Salvation Army kettles—there is a desire for "peace and goodwill" for all. Soldiers in battle have been known to lay down their arms on Christmas Eve, "so hallow'd and gracious is the time." Christmas reveals the universal spirit of love—we don't need to have wars, hate need not rule, selfishness and greed need not dominate our lives—we have a higher force within us that could change our lives and our world significantly, if we but believe in it and release it and live by it all year.

🌲🌳🌲

## *Saturday Is United Nations Day*

10-22-92

Saturday commemorates the founding of the United Nations. The United Nations Charter was signed Oct. 24, 1945. Minnesota's Harold Stassen is the sole remaining United States signator.

During the Persian Gulf War the United Nations Security Council achieved new stature and the role of the UN has been strengthening since. Although praising its functioning and urging a broadening of the role of the UN, the United States has yet to catch up on its back dues and give the UN the support it needs and deserves.

UNESCO, a research and action agency of the UN in the field of education and social services has done good work in some areas and disappointed the U. S. in others, particularly in the area of a free press and free speech. The World Health Organization, another UN agency, has brought health experts together and carried on effective campaigns against disease in Third World countries.

As we approach the 50th Anniversary of the UN it would be a good time to renew our commitment to a world organization for mutual welfare and peace. It would also be a good time to establish a Diplomacy Academy to compare with our Naval, Air Force and Army Academies. Isn't it strange that we have gone so long without doing it? Also, shouldn't we put an end to choosing any of our ambassadors on the basis of their political contributions and limit all diplomatic appointments to career. professionally trained experts?

We have lived through a century of United States economic dominance and wealth that survived extravagance, waste, blunders, even corruption. As our economic dominance wanes we can no longer afford the shortcomings of the past. We can no longer afford dollar diplomacy. We need to rely on merit of position to win cooperation and international support. Surely we can make a better institution of the United Nations, and surely we need the best possible dedication and skills in our diplomats, enhanced by training in a world class diplomacy academy. What an exciting way to prepare for the United Nations 50th anniversary in 1995.

# Celebrating A Centennial

## 12-2-92

With this issue the *Mille Lacs County Times* celebrates its 100th Anniversary. That is a long time in Minnesota history, for the state itself was only 35 years old when the *Times* produced its first issue. Life was very different then. Families were economic units, members dependent on one another in many ways, New immigrants were pouring in. The need for housing and other structures made the timber industry boom. The biggest industry in the state was grist milling and flour production.

From the beginning Mille Lacs Lake was a dominant feature of life here. Milaca, a derivative of Mille Lacs, meaning a thousand lakes. Milaca has the distinction of having the only community name in our state that is not found in any other state. It is unique.

Life in those early days was demanding. Everything was hard work and it took the major part of every family's time from dawn to dark, to produce a livelihood. Much of what was needed was home made. For fun there was hunting, fishing and trapping and happy dance parties. Church was an important center for much family                              participation.

Putting out a newspaper was no cinch either. Every word had to be spelled out one letter at a time with individual pieces of type. It was an incredibly tedious job, and then when the papers were printed the type had to be distributed in the right compartments of the type tray to be ready for the next issue. The *Times* started out as the product of a Milaca Co-op and then was taken over by Fay Craven, grandfather of Jere. Three generations of the Craven family made it a career. We did not know the first two but have been well acquainted with Jere.

From handset type the paper moved to the Linotype age where an operator could type lines of type and they were cast in lead and when used went back in the pot for melting and reuse. That was a tremendous revolution at the time but the machines were a headache to keep operating satisfactorily. Today we would think of them as Rube Goldberg affairs.

Jere Craven was one of the principals in the next major technological change with offset printing on large web presses requiring central printing plants so several publishers could band together to provide enough business to support the new technology. That was the beginning of ECM Publishers Inc. as we know it today. The first printing press that went into that plant about twenty years ago is just now being replaced.

But the real story of a paper is not the technology—it is rather the history of a community and an area. Milaca and the surrounding area has grown steadily in economic diversity and substance. Over the years the residents built a strong school system, several churches, a strong health care program and has been the beneficiary of an excellent highway program. With all the technology there is today one can hardly imagine what could develop in another century. One has to leave it to the imagination. The challenge will be to cope with an increasing population, maintain peace between nations, figuring out how to keep governmental spending and revenues in closer balance, and adjust to the changing makeup of our population.

Native Americans have been important in this area. Kathio was the capital of the Sioux Nation. Not in all their history have they enjoyed such bounty as now flows in from the casinos and gambling proceeds. A new and youthful team will be leading the nation as president and vice president and women are playing an increasing role, not only in government but in business as well. We live in an exciting time of transition when all the peoples of the world are in closer relationship than ever before. It is a time fraught with risk but also a future of the most fantastic possibilities.

*The Mille Lacs County Times* has been the reporter of the news for all the years past. It is appreciative of the support of subscribers and advertisers. We will do our best to continue reporting the life and growth of a splendid people.

🌲🌲🌲

# Observing The 100th Birthday Of The Automobile

8-12-93

Aquatore Park in Blaine will be the site of the 26th Annual Twin Cities Collectors Car Show on September 5. In addition to the 39 classes of vehicles and 121 trophies to be awarded, everyone attending will receive a commemorative folder marking the 100th anniversary of the Duryea Motor Car. It is generally agreed that the Duryea, first sold in 1893, was the first American car. The Smithsonian Institute, Washington, D.C. has one and so identifies it. It was a "horseless carriage" and designed by Charles E. Duryea.

Motor car development went on simultaneously in many countries, preceded by power driven vehicles using steam engines. Acceptance, at first, was slow. In the 1890s England had a red flag law requiring that a man walk in front of the steam driven vehicles, carrying a red flag by day and a red lantern by night. Rates for such vehicles were higher on toll roads and bridges and stopped development in England until 1896 when the red flag law was repealed.

Motor car development depended on development of the internal combustion engine. Gottfried Daimler is generally given credit for this marvel and the time about 1886, in Germany. Many pioneers worked on phases of automobile efficiency and the industry grew rapidly. Apart from those who provided the original basic inventions it was Henry Ford who made the greatest contribution to the industry's growth and established leadership for the United States.

Henry Ford built his first car in 1896. In 1902 he built the famous "999" racing roadster that he drove at 91.4 miles per hour. In 1920 came the Model T Ford, the intrepid "tin lizzie." Ford announced a new method of manufacture, the production line, and set a $5 per hour pay rate for factory workers. It was the highest pay scale at that time and caused a sensation. The Ford design, production and marketing genius put an auto within reach of every American family and mass production of automobiles had arrived. The model A Ford sedan came in 1929.

So completely did the U.S. take over the market that by 1952 it made 73% of all the passenger cars in the world and 63% of all the trucks. That continued until the 1970s when Germany and Japan made their strong moves. America's love affair with the automobile continues. Many like to own and preserve old cars and, on occasion, show them off. Many others love the nostalgia of seeing old cars ("I had one like that once") and will have their chance Sept 5.

*Individuals Remembered*

# Two-Term Presidents

## 11-15-84

When Ronald Reagan finishes his second term he will be one of 12 of our 39 presidents who have served for eight consecutive years. Four of our first five presidents did, Washington, Jefferson, Madison, Monroe were the four, John Adams our second president, did not.

From 1825 to 1901 only two presidents served through second terms, Andrew Jackson and U.S. Grant. In this century Reagan becomes the sixth. The others: Theodore Roosevelt, Woodrow Wilson, Franklin Roosevelt, Harry Truman and Dwight Eisenhower.

Grover Cleveland is a special case. He served for eight years but not consecutively. His first term was 1885 to 1889, Harrison intervened for one term and Cleveland served again from 1893 to 1897.

*Among the many fond memories of knowing Charles Lindbergh is the flying lesson he gave the author in 1969, the only one ever taken, in a float plane over the future Voyageurs National Park.*

# Lindbergh's Incredible Flight Sixty Years Ago

## 5-14-87

Seventy Minnesotans will join hundreds of others from other parts of the country for a rendezvous in Paris next week to join the French in marking the 60th anniversary of Charles A. Lindbergh's incredible flight, non-stop from New York to Paris, landing on May 21, 1927.

One of the features of a many event program will be a reenactment of the landing with a replica of the Spirit of St. Louis flying in from the west of France and landing at Le Bourget Field as Lindbergh did. Vern Jobst will be the pilot. The plane is the property of the Experimental Aircraft Association of Oshkosh and is being disassembled and flown to France where it will be reassembled and prepared for flight.

Lindbergh was an instant world hero. In his later years he would say—"They'll never let me fly beyond Paris." He was 25 when he made his famous flight and 72 when he died in 1974. In the intervening 47 years he made many contributions much of which is little remembered now. He and Dr. Alexis Carrel were featured on the cover of *Time* magazine for their collaboration and successful development of a perfusion Pump that is the basis today for organ transplant surgery.

It was Charles Lindbergh who heard about the physics professor who had an idea that a rocket could be devised with the potential of projecting beyond the pull of gravity and traveling into space even to the extent of landing on the moon. Few people gave credence to such an idea but Lindbergh was impressed after a visit with Robert Goddard and encouraged his friend Harry Frank Guggenheim and the Guggenheim Foundation to fund Goddard's experiments for five years and later provide him with test sites in New Mexico. That was the beginning of the space program.

Following his solo flight Lindbergh and his wife, Anne, worked with TWA and Pan American in charting the first international plane routes to Europe, Asia and South America. Much could be written about Anne Lindbergh who became a full partner of her husband as a skilled radio operator and navigator—mothered six children and wrote 13 books. Her *Gift From The Sea* is a classic no one should miss.

During World War II Lindbergh flew bombing missions in the South Pacific as a civilian consultant teaching pilots to increase fuel efficiency by raising compression and reducing rpm. Recently a World War II fighter pilot told me he owed his life to Lindbergh because of that training. He was on a mission and just barely made it back which he would have been unable to do without the added flight time Lindbergh's training provided.

Lindbergh wrote an account of his flight, *The Spirit of St. Louis* which won a Pulitzer Prize. As he grew older Lindbergh became increasingly concerned with the protection of the environment and limitations on technology's ability to solve all problems. He became a world leader in the protection of endangered species of wildlife. He felt there had to be a balance between having the benefits of technology and preserving the environment and the quality of life. This philosophy was outlined in a little book, *Of Flight and Life,* published in 1948 and in much more detail in *Autobiography of Values* which he had arranged to be published after his death.

He was a frequent visitor to Minnesota, his home state, and followed the restoration of the family home at Little Falls with interest as well as the development of the Museum in the Lindbergh State Park. He aided in the establishment of Voyageurs National Park which he thought one of the great parks of the world because of the water orientation.

When he learned he was dying of cancer he arranged transportation to Maui, Hawaii where he wanted to die and be buried. He had come to love its beauty and its people. He asked some of his friends to make a "box" for him to be buried in, which they did with loving care, of eucalyptus wood. He did not want his body embalmed and permission was granted if he would be interred within eight hours of death. This precluded any big burial service. He also stipulated that he be buried in Maui work clothes.

His body rests in a tiny church yard in Kipahulu with an inscription on a headstone which reads, "If I take the wings of the morning and dwell in the uttermost parts of the sea." If you read the 139th Psalm the verse acquires meaning and reveals the testimony of his life.

★ 🌲 ★

*The author's service as Minnesota's 30th governor coincided with most of John F. Kennedy's presidency.*

# Recollections of President John F. Kennedy

7-7-88

In this 25th anniversary year of his death many articles are recalling the life of President John F. Kennedy. There are three experiences that come to my mind.

In 1960 as a possible candidate for governor of Minnesota I was invited to attend the Gridiron Banquet in Washington where the press has a field day in lampooning top officials who have their chance to slam right back. It is an hilarious evening of wit and entertainment.

At the 1960 event it happened that the Minnesota delegation was placed next to the Massachusetts delegation and I was seated right next to John Kennedy. This was our first meeting. He was then campaigning in the Wisconsin primary against Hubert Humphrey and seemed eager to talk politics with a Minnesotan.

Up to that time there had been discussion of the youthfulness of Kennedy and whether he was mature enough to be president. He affected a haircut with a slightly tousled effect that made him look younger than his 43 years and had a youthful life style. My reaction after that evening's visit was to return to Minnesota and tell friends, "This fellow is fully mature—don't have any illusions about that." It was so obvious that growing up with a family deeply involved in tough Massachusetts, national and international politics had fully prepared him. He proved his mettle in the campaign and in the presidency where he might be characterized as cool and tough in his dealings with others.

Another experience was during the Cuban missile crisis. Pictures from high flying aircraft disclosed that Cuba had missiles in launching sites aimed at the U.S. Russia had been shipping in large amounts of war material until, with one convoy on its way, Kennedy informed Russia that it must turn back or face an encounter with the U. S. Navy which had instructions not to permit the ships to land.

The civil defense committee of the governors of which Nelson Rockefeller of New York was chairman and I a member was called to the White House for consultations and briefing. We were shown the photo which, when enlarged, left no doubt of the threat erected in Cuba. We were told flatly that should Russia fail to turn back, war could be the result. Kennedy was resolute and calm, confident that Russia would not persist in its program. It was a tense time until word came that the Russian ships had reversed course and the crisis averted.

A few days after his death I was traveling in Central America. The shock and sorrow at the assassination was every bit as marked there as at home. Memorial services were held and people were in tears. Kennedy had become an idol and a model with his confident, youthful breezy style, his beautiful wife, his knowledge of Spanish. Not in anyone's memory had a U.S. president so impressed himself on the consciousness and affection of the Latin American people as had Kennedy.

Recollections of his popularity remain strong, stature of his accomplishments have declined. There is not necessarily a perfect correlation, if any, between a president's popularity while in office, and the considered value of his incumbency to the nation long range. President John Kennedy was clearly a leader who could inspire, as in his inaugural address, and could face the challenges of difficult decisions as he did on more than one occasion.

🌲🌲🌲🌲

# One Individual Who Made A Difference

## 8-4-88

Francis Scott Key, whose birthdate Aug. 1, 1779 we recognize this week, was a lawyer-social worker who also happened to be something of a poet. While he was on a legal mission his ship was anchored off Baltimore, held up by the British bombardment of Fort McHenry during the night of Sept. 13–14, 1814. At daybreak he was so thrilled to see the American flag still flying over the fort that he was inspired to write a poem. He sent it to the Baltimore Sun which published it. In time it was set to music (not so inspired) but it was 117 years later, when President Herbert Hoover approved the legislation, that it officially became our national anthem, "The Star Spangled Banner."

Key probably little realized the importance of his poem at the time he wrote it. Inspiration is a powerful force that works through humankind when individuals release it.

🌲🌳🌲

# Which Bush Will Be President?

11-17-88

When George Bush became known to most people as vice president he was a deferential careful person, very conscious of his secondary and supportive role relative to the president. Some people began to call him a wimp when he sought the presidential nomination, which my brand new Random House dictionary defines as a weak, ineffectual, dull person.

That identification, if it ever applied, lost all significance when Bush made his acceptance speech at the Republican National Convention. A strong, new, aggressive Bush appeared who made a dynamic speech and took off for the presidency like a rocket. He gave the clue when he said he had a mission and he was determined to fulfill it.

His campaign was too assertive and combative for the taste of many voters but it had its effect. Is that the Bush who will be president?

There was another Bush, the pre-1980 Bush. The Bush who served in many important offices, quietly, effectively, known to his friends as a courageous but not aggressive person, a caring man, one who gathered a large core of admiring friends who had high hopes for his future—the highest.

That was the Bush I met when he came to Minnesota in 1978 to speak at a fund raiser for Al Quie at a private residence in White Bear Lake. Al Quie was running for the governorship at the time, which he won.

On our way home that evening I remarked that for the first time in a long time I had met a person with the intellectual capacity, the character, the style, the education and training, the experience that made him truly worthy to be a president of the United States. We supported him in 1980. He was considered too liberal for the mood of the party and the times and the nomination went to Ronald Reagan. There was grumbling among the conservatives when Bush emerged as the vice presidential candidate. Bush carried the difficult role with just the balance that enabled him to keep his own identity and individuality while serving the president.

It is that pre-1980 person that I believe will now emerge as the president—to lead a "gentler and kinder nation" into years of profound difficulty for our country. It is reflected in his wife who will bring character and charm to her role as first lady, and in the Bush's relationships with their children and grandchildren.

*Val Bjornson, served as State Treasurer during the tenure of six governors, including that of the author.*

## Kristjan Valdimar Bjornson Dies

### 3-19-87

Last week Tuesday Minnesota lost one of its noblest citizens with the passing, at age 80, of former State Treasurer Val Bjornson.

If only one word was permitted to describe a man, we would pick "steadfast" for Val. It's a fine old English word that goes back hundreds of years. It is currently defined as "fixed in direction, steadily directed, firm, as in purpose and resolution, firmly established, as an institution or a state of affairs, firmly fixed in place or position." Some of the synonyms listed are: sure, dependable, reliable, constant, unwavering, undeviating constancy or resolution. That was Val.

A humble man, he was not boastful of his accomplishment, few knew that he graduated from the University of Minnesota summa cum laude and was named a member of Phi Beta Kappa, honorary academic fraternity, and Delta Sigma Rho, honorary forensic society.

He served in the Navy in world War II, stationed in Iceland where he met his wife Gudrun and was discharged with the rank of Lieutenant Commander.

He was elected and re-elected State Treasurer for 22 years bringing dignity and respect to that office. Former State Public Examiner Ray Vecellio told us, at the memorial service, "I audited his books for many years and there never was a single irregularity."

Val was born in tiny Minnesota, in Lyon County, where his father

Gunnar Bjornson was publisher and editor of the *Minnesota Mascot* and where all members of the large family worked during their school years. Val started at 12 and journalism was his craft when he was not in public service.

History and linguistics commanded Val's deep interest. He produced a four volume history of Minnesota. For years he broadcast a radio program on WCAL reviewing Scandinavian news every Sunday morning.

He was in constant demand for commencement addresses and commemorative occasions. He had a deep impressive voice. His rich vocabulary which he used so effectively coupled with a knowledge of history that always brought new light on any subject made all of his his speaking dates occasions to enjoy and remember. The heroic dimension he brought as public speaker informed and inspired countless audiences.

But steadfastness of character and personality is what we come back to—steadfast in appreciation of his Icelandic heritage, steadfast in devotion to a wife and large family of promising children and grandchildren, steadfast in a public service of integrity and unselfishness—steadfast in a friendship that was vast—steadfast in the faith of his fathers as a member of Grace University Lutheran Church for more than a half century.

Minnesota, and his family, have suffered a loss in the death of Kristjan Valdimar Bjornson but can always retain the memory of his life with pride.

# John Milton Born Dec. 9, 1608

## 12-7-89

It was 381 years ago this week that John Milton, the great English poet, champion of freedom of the press, and human rights was born. It was Milton who said: "No man who knows aught can be so stupid as to deny that all men naturally were born free." Today, nothing is more current than the struggle for that inherent right.

🌲🌳🌳🌲

*Exemplifying the irresistible identification of Minnesotans with the vast North country and its rich history in exploration are the North and South Pole expeditions of Will Steger of Ely.*

# Why Did Will Steger Do It?

## 5-24-90

What was the point of men and dogs trekking across 3700 miles of Antarctica's forbidding environment of snow, cold and biting winds? Was it limited to a dramatic challenge of nature? In an informative, inspiring and at times deeply moving lecture at the University of Minnesota last Wednesday Will Steger told of the environmental and educational goals of the effort.

Like many people Steger has had a concern about the deterioration of our earth environment and given much thought to what should be done and what he could contribute.

His first conclusion was that if something important was to be accomplished it would have to be international. Almost all environmental problems are international in impact and solution. He felt that tackling a relatively easier international project might be a way of bringing worldwide concern and action into focus. Then, as a teacher, he decided that reaching the school children of the world might be the best way to reach all people or at least generate future results if not immediate.

To undertake to save the earth, he reasoned, Antarctica might be a good place to start, crossing the continent by dog team which was his specialty, would be a way to command the attention of youth particularly, and doing it with an international team of experts would draw worldwide attention.

That was the concept. It took $8 million to accomplish and it meant incredible effort to win financial support for the idea and confidence in the possibility of success. Concurrent with fund raising, preparations went forward, not only for the infinite detail of planning for the trip itself, but the development and publication of educational materials to distribute to school children around the world, to arrange telecommunication and radio hookups so the trip's progress could be communicated. Included was the publishing of a comprehensive guide to "Saving the Earth".

What manner of man is this who could dream such a dream, and have the strength and fortitude to carry it forward? Steger is nothing if not completely honest and straight forward. There is no pretense, no sign of ego, but the gradual revelation of enormous inner resources of strength, commitment, determination, positive thinking and confidence. There may be barriers but nothing insurmountable.

One might expect to meet a large powerfully built individual but quite the opposite was the case. Steger is of average height and of moderate build. He came in well used outdoor type slacks, open collar shirt, and pullover sweater. He talked quietly, informally, but with complete command of his material and smoothly articulate expression. His demeanor was serious, but occasionally a warm open smile brightened his countenance. One could not help but be drawn to him and his cause in complete confidence, he has that mystical magnetism of the true leader.

His mission—to save Antarctica as the beginning of a worldwide effort and commitment to save the earth that is our home. Antarctica is a relatively simple problem. It has been spared major development so far, no nation has an enormous investment there. But no time is to be lost. An international treaty is under consideration to provide for exploratory mineral drilling. The Steger position, let's just save Antarctica as it is—let us do nothing there but limited carefully controlled tourism, carefully planned research, but no exploitation. It should be possible and if successful would generate the foundation of cooperation that could be turned to other projects.

At one point during the trip when many days of storm and bitter cold were threatening, Steger's confidence did not waver. He said he thought of all the kids around the world who were following the trip. He said with that joining of human spirit they simply could not fail, that power would see them through.

Steger believes progress begins with individuals but when many join together in common purpose of noble dimension a spiritual strength is generated that is not to be denied. Minnesota can be proud that it produced a leader of the character of Will Steger. He has taken on one of the biggest world issues of our time and we have probably only started to sense the measure of his own impact on the 21st century.

# Frank Lloyd Wright Lives On

### 6-7-90

Although Frank Lloyd Wright, one of America's greatest architects, died more than 30 years ago, his influence lives on. Regularly his name is in the news, because one of his homes or buildings is bring preserved, his style is being reflected in new work, or someone refers to him and his accomplishments. He was outspoken and often critical of architectural work that had preceded him and left many good quotes. One memorable observation: "No house should ever be built on a hill or on anything. It should be of the hill, belonging to it, so hill and house could live together each the happier for the other." Wright was born June 8, 1867 and died April 9, 1959.

★♣♣★

# Judith Ann (Heart Warrior) Chosa:
# A Voice From The Boundary Waters

### 9-6-90

Her home is a four to six hour paddle and portage from Ely on Basswood Lake. She is an independent candidate for governor. She is a college trained, published author, 44 year old mother of an 11 year old son, one of two remaining Native Americans of the Ojibwe (Chippewa) tribe still living in the Boundary Waters Canoe Area. She writes eloquent prose in a column for the *Ely Echo* entitled "A voice from the Boundary Waters." She is worthy of attention. Her name is Judith Ann (Heart Warrior) Chosa.

## A Refreshingly Clear Platform

Heart Warrior makes her position clear on major issues. She is deeply concerned for the northern Minnesota watershed, threatened by the prospect of heavy mineral mining. For women she is pro-choice and for pay equity. She favors an elders council. "Our Elders are wise and I listen," she says. She also feels people of color are underrepresented in the legislature and other governmental bodies and so recommends a People of Color Council "All people must be represented."

## Crisis In The Watershed

Minnesota's watershed in the Boundary Waters Canoe Area is the largest, cleanest freshwater source on the continent, is dispersed in all directions affecting a third of the people on the continent, Heart Warrior points out, and is now threatened by state policy and mining greed. Since 1985, 34 companies have leased more than 600 tracts of land for exploratory drilling in some areas close to the Boundary Waters Canoe Area. An additional group is to be offered for bids on Oct. 4. The main search is for copper/nickel deposits, but it is no secret that gold is also on the agenda. If the world market for gold reached $500 an ounce, it is said, mining would begin in Minnesota.

Heart Warrior points out that heavy minerals such as those sought are found in sulfide deposits and their removal is far different from iron mining. Sulphuric or sulphurous acid can be released into the downstream waters and there is no known technology for clearing it once the pollution occurs. Minnesota laws are simply not in shape to provide adequate controls on the mining of heavy minerals even though years of exploration have gone on. The interest of the mining companies is unabated and full scale production could be launched almost any time.

## *A Mystical Bond With Water*

It is from deep in her American Indian heritage that Chosen Warrior draws her impassioned concern for the watershed that has been the home of her people for hundreds, maybe thousands of years. Recently she wrote in the *Ely Echo*: "My lake, my mother's shielding arms, who is this wretch that seeks to steal you from me? Who is this swine gold hunter that would kill you? How can it be so? What kind of blindness is it that does not see your sacredness? Mother, take me to your heart and tell your clumsy child it is not true or else tell me what to do. Name it, I will do anything. All your children are like you. Strong, enduring against all odds, invincible like the mighty mothering shield you are. What is it we may do for you? Your hand and it alone will give the blessing. We know your body houses all that is sacred. Speak, whisper holy words that I might understand. You are invincible. It is known."

Judith Ann (Heart Warrior) Chosa brings important information to the 1990 election campaign in Minnesota and it is to be hoped her concern for the watershed will be shared by legislators who will work to get our laws in shape. If, as Chosa discovered, it is possible there are mineral rights owned in the Boundary Waters Canoe Area, they should be revealed and acquired by the state without further delay.

# Geoffrey Chaucer:
## He Died In 1400, But Lives On

### 10-28-90

This week is the 590th anniversary of the death of Geoffrey Chaucer. He had a varied career but is primarily remembered as a poet, author of *Canterbury Tales,* the fascinating story of 23 pilgrims journeying from London to the shrine of St. Thomas a Becket at Canterbury. The pilgrims were an interesting cross section of humankind, wonderfully sketched and etched by Chaucer. They made up stories to pass the time along the way. The result—17,000 lines of poetry—a vivid depiction of medieval attitudes toward love, marriage, religion and the human condition. The work was forgotten for 400 years but was rediscovered in the 19th century, reprinted in both prose and poetry versions and continues to be reprinted today. Any bookstore would have a copy in some form and it is delightful reading.

Chaucer is now acclaimed as one of the great English authors and Chaucer's *Canterbury Tales* a masterpiece. Today, 600 years later, you'll recognize the pilgrims as people you know.

# Anniversary Of Will Rogers Birth

### 11-1-90

His full name was William Penn Adair Rogers and he was born in Oologah Indian Territory (now Oklahoma) on Nov. 4, 1879. He became one of America's most loved entertainers as he twirled his rope and drawled one fascinating observation after another. He once said "My forefathers didn't come over on the Mayflower—they met the boat." He it was who also said: "I belong to no organized political party—I'm a Democrat." Can you imagine what the political situation in Minnesota this week might have inspired him to say?

🌲🌳🌲

## Archbishop Rembert Weakland: A Service To All America

### 10-5-86

Archbishop Rembert G. Weakland of Milwaukee rendered a service to all Americans when he took issue with the Pope recently in columns Weakland wrote for his archdiocesan newspaper.

Although not named, readers concluded that Weakland was commenting on the removal of authority from Archbishop Raymond G. Hunthausen of Seattle because of the Pope's disagreement with some of his practices and statements and more especially to the Papal action barring the Rev. Charles E. Curran from further teaching at the Catholic University of America in Washington D.C. because of the nature of his views.

Weakland called on his church to "avoid the fanaticism and small-mindedness that has characterized so many periods of the church in its history—tendencies that lead to much cruelty, suppression of theological creativity and lack of growth."

If a non Catholic were to say that there could be quick dismissal of the observation as anti-Catholic, but it cannot be dismissed when Archbishop Weakland says it. He is acknowledged as one of the leading scholars of the church and most influential in the community of Catholic bishops in America. He is chairman of the committee drafting a letter on the economy and is a past head of the Benedictine Order, worldwide.

Weakland recalled the words of Pope John XXIII when he said the church "meets the needs of the present day by demonstrating the validity of her teaching rather than by condemnations."

All Americans can be grateful for the admonishment of Milwaukee's courageous archbishop: "the church must always face up to the challenges of the times and the new discoveries about the universe and the human person."

🌲🌲🌲🌲

# *Wolfgang Amadeus Mozart*

## 1-31-91

In the judgment of many, Mozart was the greatest musical genius who ever lived. He died 200 years ago this year, in poverty, and was buried in a pauper's grave. Throughout this year there will be concerts, memorial programs, and every kind of tribute, but while he lived his musical contributions could not earn him a decent living.

"Beauty of sound, classical grace, technical perfection" are some of the phrases used to characterize his work. Elegance, may be as good a term as any. While he lived innovation, invention, complication were some of the reactions expressed.

He was born into a musical family and at 3 showed musical aptitude. At 5 he was already composing and performing. His musical development was rapid but either out of jealousy or for whatever reason he never received a post worthy of his talents, The last 10 years of his life, from 25 to 35 have been regarded as the most productive in musical history. At one point he composed three major works in six weeks. Some of his greatest compositions he never heard performed. He composed in every musical genre—concertos, sonatas, symphonies, opera—everything. No one to equal him has ever appeared since.

How futile it is to honor a great human being long after death, particularly when that enormous human resource was not fully appreciated while he or she lived. We can only express gratitude that there are individuals so talented, noble and persevering that despite rebuffs continue lives of creativity and contribution to the very end, however difficult that may be.

# Thomas H. Swain

7-9-92

It is people like Tom Swain who keep a society functioning and growing. Gov. Arne Carlson has just named him to be Chair of the commission provided for in the HealthRight Law. That commission will be working with Commissioner Natalie Steffen and the Department of Human Services to institute the new program designed to bring health care protection to people of the state not now covered. It is also expected to bring a report to the Governor and the Legislature in January with recommendations for containing costs, improving services, and generally enhancing the functioning of the health care industry in Minnesota.

That is a tremendous assignment. No other state has undertaken what Minnesota is now embarked upon, but all have the same need and will watch our progress. The human and cost impacts are so great that success will be an enormous victory. For years special interests have influenced legislation, pricing procedures, and every other element of health care with selfish interest in mind as well as effective care for the patient. There is surely room for improvement but it will take courage to address issues plainly and openly, and dedication to the public interest to get some changes made.

It was just a short time ago that Swain was asked to take charge of the insurance fund involved with the workers compensation law which was in a sad state of disarray. For more than thirty years he has been serving the public interest as well as having a career with the St. Paul Companies. He is relatively unknown to the general public but it is doubtful if there is another person in the state who has been involved in as many social service, educational, cultural and governmental agencies in as important ways as he. As a leader in the effort to improve the manner of selecting regents of the University of Minnesota, he fostered the legislation, and has been a member of the Regent Candidate Advisory Council from its beginning. He is now a vice chairman and has contributed substantially to its success. He is a board member of the Schubert Club. He has been on the board of the Citizens League for many years and served as president and in other capacities.

One of his associates has said, "He has the best organized mind of anyone I ever knew." He is of impeccable integrity, diligent, selfless, faithful to every trust, and dedicated to making the American dream come true for everyone through private and public operations of the highest ethical standards. Minnesota is lucky to have him available and willing to take on his most important challenge.

🌲🌲🌲🌲

# Remembering Emily Dickinson

12-9-93

Emily Dickinson is now recognized as one of the greatest lyric poets in the English language. It has been a developing recognition. She was born Dec. 10, 1830 in Amherst, Massachusetts. She never married, lived in the family home her entire life. For 20 years she cared for both her father and mother as their health failed and until their death.

Very few of her poems were published in her lifetime, and then by editors who could not accept her innovations and edited them. After her death her sister found a box of more than 2000 poems, mostly only a few lines long, and apparently written on whatever bits of paper happened to be handy. Books of her poems were published after her death but usually edited and changed. Years later, in 1955, Harvard University Press published a three volume edition of her poetry in the form she wrote them and this has become the standard.

Her personal life, her inner life, was not as tranquil as the setting might suggest. She experienced intense emotion and had years of personal turmoil. She walked and observed nature as an outlet, thought profoundly on many subjects. Whatever she wrote before age 28 has been lost, but about that time she decided that what she was writing might have worth and preserved it. Her efforts to interest publishers found little encouragement. She died May 15, 1886 without the recognition she deserved. Now, 100 years later she and her work are cherished. Many biographies have been written as well as critical appraisals, to supplement the Harvard collection of her work. Here are three samples of her poetry:

*Aristocracy*
*The pedigree of honey*
*Does not concern the bee;*
*A clover, any time, to him*
*Is aristocracy.*

*Autumn*
*The morns are meeker than they were,*
*The nuts are getting brown;*
*The berry's cheek is plumper,*
*The rose is out of town.*
*The maple wears a gayer scarf,*
*The field a scarlet gown. Lest I should be old-fashioned,*
*I'll put a trinket on.*

*There Is No Frigate Like A Book*
*There is no frigate like a book*
*To take us lands away,*
*Nor any coursers like a page*
*Of prancing poetry.*

*The traverse may the poorest take*
*Without oppress of toil; How frugal is the chariot*
*That bears a human soul!*

🌲🌳🌳🌲

# Historians Will Remember Richard Nixon

### 4-28-94

Not all people will mourn the passing of former President Richard M. Nixon, but historians will remember him. He had courage but not much charisma. His understanding of international relations was not matched by his understanding of people. He left the presidency in disgrace but made decisions of epochal importance.

He was president at a time when there was strong anti-Communist sentiment in the country. He had been part of that movement. He had a confrontation with Nikita Krushchev in Moscow that may well be decided as marking the turning point in Soviet unbridled expansion. He stood up to Krushchev's temper tantrum and bizarre pounding the table with his shoe and talked him down.

At the same time he dealt differently with another communist nation—China. He recognized with vision ahead of his contemporaries that China would play an enormous role in the 21st Century and the whole Asia-Pacific area was of tremendous significance. He felt that a rapprochement with China and a renewal of diplomatic relations was essential, and accomplished it. A Democrat president could have hardly risked the charges of "soft on Communism" but no one could make that charge against Nixon. He accomplished a tremendously important accommodation at an important time.

Nixon visited Minnesota in the 1960 campaign. He and his wife Pat made a whistle stop train tour from Fargo-Moorhead to Minneapolis. He lost Minnesota by 22,000 votes—Kennedy's 779,000 to Nixon's 757,000, one of the smallest presidential differences in Minnesota history. Rhoda Lund, National Committee woman for the Republican party and her husband, Russell, were personal friends of the Nixons and aided them in many ways.

Nixon seemed cold and aloof to some people but among those who knew him his intellectual capacity, his vision for the nation, and commitment to the country's best interest was unquestioned. As with many presidents before and since, the contemporary evaluation will not be the final one.

⁂

*The author had the privilege of serving on the 1958 Statehood Centennial committee that commissioned a statue of Maria Sanford for placement in Statuary Hall in the nation's capitol.*

# Maria Sanford, A True Symbol Of Minnesota

### 3-9-95

A visit to Washington provides many opportunities. For Minnesotans it can include Evelyn Raymond's magnificent 6'11" heroic sculpture of Maria Sanford located near the main entrance to the Senate Chamber.

Each state was given an opportunity of honoring two of its citizens with full figure sculptures to be placed in various locations of the capitol building. Minnesota's first honoree was Henry M Rice, delegate to the Territorial Assembly, early political leader and one of our first two U.S. Senators. It was not until the 1939 legislative session, under the leadership of Harold Stassen, that a resolution was passed designating educator Maria Sanford as the second person to be honored. In 1957, in a bill to finance celebrating the state's centennial, funds were provided to carry out the 1939 resolution.

A commission was established and Evelyn Raymond was chosen from a large field of sculptor applicants. There was a noble simplicity about her model that impressed the commission as appropriate to the subject and presenting her, holding a book, as representing Minnesota values. A dedication ceremony was held at the Capitol with Guy Stanton Ford, former Dean of the Graduate School and President of the University of Minnesota, as the principal speaker. Maria Sanford was only the second woman to be so honored (Frances E. Willard of Illinois was the first) and Minnesotans can always be proud of her choice.

She was born in Saybrook, Connecticut on Dec. 19, 1836. Her love of education was early evident; at 16 she was teaching in country day schools. She used dowry funds to pay tuition at Connecticut Normal School. She became a school principal, county superintendent at Chester County, Pennsylvania and Professor of History at Swarthmore College, one of the first woman professors in the country. When invited to join the University of Minnesota faculty, she responded enthusiastically and was professor of Rhetoric and Elocution from 1880 to 1909. She lectured on literature and art history, she was a champion of women's rights, supported the education of blacks, and was a pioneer of adult education. She traveled throughout the country giving more than 1000 patriotic speeches, the most famous being a powerful address "An Apostrophe to the Flag." She died April 21, 1920 at 83, "the best loved woman of the North Star State."

## Msgr. Yzermans Passing
## A Sad Loss For Many

5-11-95

It is appropriate that memorial services for the departed celebrate their lives and contributions. So it is for Msgr. Vincent A. Yzermans, who died in a nursing home in Albuquerque, New Mexico last Thursday. In his case, however, relationships were so particularly personal, so deep and long established that a great many people will mourn his death for a long time.

Msgr. Yzermans, a native of St. Paul, educated at Crozier Seminary, Notre Dame and Fordham Universities was first and foremost, and for 44 years, a priest of the Roman Catholic Church. He served a number of parishes and the St. Cloud Diocese in many ways. He was a warm, understanding, compassionate spiritual leader. He lifted people's vision, inspired their efforts and comforted them in trial and grief. His empathy enabled him to relate to all with whom he came in contact. It was not always easy. He sometimes felt he was part of a "lost generation" of priests, too liberal for their older more conservative colleagues and not liberal enough for the younger priests coming on.

He was a research scholar and prodigious writer. Even in his latter years when he was attached to an oxygen tank many hours a day, his productivity was incredible. In the introduction to *Gatherings* published in late 1993 he wrote: "For twenty-two months I worked night and day on my memoirs. In God's good time—for all time is God's good time—they may someday be published either while I am still in the land of the living or sharing more fully in the glory of God. That will be His Holy will." His memoirs, *Journeys* was published last year.

James and Dorothy Blommer of the Park Press, St. Cloud, who were responsible for getting many of Msgr. Yzermans' books into print, published, as a Christmas book, last December, *From St. Nicholas to Santa Claus*. It is a carefully researched and fascinatingly written account of the origins and development of the modern Santa Claus figure, from the original beloved prelate, St. Nicholas. An example of his creative imagination was the fantasy of the youthful Jesus' trip to Rome and visit with the Emperor. He wrote histories of Elk River and Cambridge parishes, of the St. Cloud Diocese, a biography of the first Bishop of St. Cloud and hundreds of articles. He wanted to leave a legacy and indeed he did. His life and work will be rippling through history for a long time, and he will live on in the memories of his loving friends.

*One of three Minnesotans to serve on the United States Supreme Court and the only one to serve as Chief Justice (1969–86).*

# Warren Burger, Now A Cherished Memory

### 6-29-95

Former U. S. Supreme Court Chief Justice died last Sunday in Washington at 87. It will be left to legal scholars to analyze and appraise his actions and opinions as Court of Appeals judge and later Chief Justice. His friends in Minnesota will cherish the memory of its native son as a man of fine character who with talent applied hard work, stability and persistence to rise from a modest East side St. Paul home to the highest judicial post in the nation.

It is said that in his school years he was offered a scholarship at a prominent eastern school. As the oldest child in the family he felt a duty to stay home, work and contribute to the family finances which he did. He studied law at night at St. Paul's Wm. Mitchell Law School, graduated and was admitted to the bar. While practicing law he became interested in Republican party politics and the career of Harold Stassen. Burger distinguished himself with his keen analytical mind, his sound judgment, the stability of his character and the breadth of his understanding and vision. He also had an appearance, a bearing and a persuasive speaking style that won respect and adherents.

A decisive point in his career occurred at the 1952 Republican National Convention where Burger served on the Credentials Committee. He pleaded the case of a rump delegation from Texas, which was for Eisenhower, and secured its recognition over the regular delegation which was for Taft. That switch, plus the move of Minnesota from Stassen to Eisenhower decided the nomination. Burger had worked closely with Herbert Brownell, who became Attorney General and invited Burger to Washington as an assistant. He was appointed to the Circuit Court of Appeals by President Dwight Eisenhower and to Chief Justice by President Richard Nixon.

Because he was a Republican Nixon appointee the media could never get over thinking of him as a conservative. He was a typical Minnesota pragmatic—progressive, responsible on fiscal and economic matters but sensitive, caring, concerned and progressive on education, welfare and social concerns. He was one of Minnesota's best, distinguishing himself wherever he went and all the time a warm and abiding friend.

🌲🌳🌳🌲

*The first governor of Minnesota from the Iron Range whose tenure of 10 years as 34th and 36th governors is the longest of any of the state's 37 chief executives (1976–79, 1983–91).*

# Rudy Perpich: The Idea Man Is Gone

9-28-95

A few days after his death, a cartoonist depicted former governor Rudy Perpich arriving at the Pearly Gates with a packet of ideas under his arm for improving Heaven. St. Peter is shown saying, "The idea man is here!" For us, the idea man is gone, and it is a significant public, and for a host of people, a personal loss.

Rudy Perpich was the son of immigrant Croatian parents who worked hard to provide their children with education and professional careers. Their background strongly influenced son Rudy's later life. He not only supported public education, he had innovative ideas for improving it. He felt it should not be lock-step, treating every child the same. He felt there should be special schools for those particularly interested and talented in art, science and math, music and other specialties. If a child and his or her parents felt another school district or school was more appropriate the child should be free to change enrollment. If a student has unusual ability that qualified him or her for University classes, the way should be open to take those classes, while still in grade or high school. Perpich ideas ruffled feathers and generated controversy but caught the attention of President George Bush and became a part of national policy.

Perpich also had ideas about public welfare. He favored generous help for those suffering hardship, but public assistance should not become a way of life. He felt state and federal regulations had the effect of entrapping people in poverty, restricting people's desire and effort to get off welfare.

Congress was persuaded to waive regulations to let Minnesota try its new approach. It has worked and been supported by successor Gov. Arne Carlson.

Perpich had some ideas about improving opportunity for women and people of color. He appointed more of them to executive and judicial positions than any governor before him. Through his appointments to the state Supreme Court he made it the first in the country to have a majority of women. He wanted everyone to have full opportunity to develop to their full potential.

His ideas were not limited by state boundaries. He was world minded and felt all our people needed to think globally and prepare for international participation. Fortunately located in the center of the North American continent and neatly half-way between Europe and Asia it was obvious to him we should have a world trade center. He also wanted a world research center here, and although they created a tremendous media event, his cast of characters, Mikhail Gorbachev and Robert Maxwell, were not the ones to accomplish it. But if Edmonton could have a super-mall, Minnesota should have a bigger one, and so Rudy promoted the Mall of America. He thought of Minnesota as the brainpower state which should be the biggest and best in everything.

Sports did not escape his attention. Of course the Superbowl should be played here, and the Final Four of the collegiate national basketball tournament. He even introduced bocce ball as a new sport. One could go on and on. Anyone as innovative, creative and provocative as he was is bound to create controversy. He was ridiculed about the chopstick factory, but even that was on track. Of Minnesota's abundant natural resources, our forestry resource is least well developed and productive and he was trying to do something about it.

Fundamentally he cared about people as individuals and was at his best and happiest when listening and chatting with them at coffee counters around the state. At times he would run away from the capitol, his staff, and the media, just to be out by himself with the people he loved and respected. He touched and inspired lives in uncounted ways. He had ideas for himself, too. There was no doubt in his mind he could be president of the United States and give the nation effective leadership.

He was honest, he worked hard for what he believed best for the state and its people. He put a confident, positive slant on opportunities. He was loyal to his friends, faithfully devoted to his wife and family, was courageous, candid and genuine. He leaves a legacy of influence and accomplishment of which any governor of Minnesota could be proud.

♣ ♣♣ ♣

## *Peter Popovich, Now A Treasured Memory*

4-4-96

Former legislator, Chief Judge of the Minnesota Appeals Court, Chief Justice of the Supreme court Peter Popovich died last Friday evening at age 75. One of the most brilliant, public spirited, productive citizens in Minnesota history, he believed in open process, fair, humane government and individual achievement based on effort and application. His was a joyful zest for life, a love of competition and the challenge of problem solving. He had a great capacity for friendship. He was born on the Iron Range of an immigrant Yugoslav family. He was proud of his origins and ethnic heritage. He went from Chisholm high school and Hibbing Junior College to the University of Minnesota, to the predecessor of the Wm. Mitchell Law School and to the establishment of the Peterson Popovich law firm. It specialized in education public finance and aided many school districts with their building programs. He was elected to the state House of Representatives in the early fifties and quickly established his leadership and aimed for the powerful chairmanship of the Appropriations Committee. An incident kept him from it and opened the way to his judicial career. During the St. Paul Winter Carnival of 1956 he was Vulcanus

67

Rex, the leader of the crew that gamboled around town, bursting in on public gatherings to smudge unsuspecting women and swear kneeling men to loyalty to Vulcan over King Boreas. On one occasion they stormed into a meeting where the governor and first lady were in attendance. Never one to be intimidated, Vulcan Peter smudged First Lady Jane Freeman. Gov. Orville Freeman was incensed, thought it highly inappropriate to submit his wife to such an indignity. Popovich attributed that incident to his denial of the Appropriations Committee chairmanship.

Fellow Iron Ranger Gov. Rudy Perpich named him Chief Judge of the new Appeals Court where Popovich established a tradition of expeditious handling of cases that made it the best court of its kind in the country. Still today it is the only appeals court with no backlog. Gov. Perpich also named him Chief Justice of the Supreme Court where he served until mandatory retirement five years ago. His last years were spent with the Briggs and Morgan law firm of St. Paul. Peter Popovich will ever be an inspiration and a treasured memory.

🌲🌲🌲

## *A Birthday Party For Willard Munger*

1-11-96

Rep. Willard M. Munger (DFL) Duluth has represented his district in the state legislature for 40 years. He is tied with Walter E. Day for longest service in the House of Representatives in our state's history. On the Senate side Donald O. Wright and A.J.

Rockne are tied at 36 years. For total legislative service in both houses, Wright and Carl Iverson are tied at 44 years; Munger is the longest-tenured still living, still serving legislator in the history of the state. On Jan. 20 he will be 85 years old. On Thursday Jan. 18, at 3 P.M. there will be a birthday party and program in the House chamber, followed by a reception and refreshments in the rotunda area. There is no charge and the public is invited.

Age and tenure are just the beginning of the Munger legend. He was born in Fergus Falls and his paternal grandfather imbued in him an appreciation, respect and reverence for the environment—water, air, the soil, the plants and trees, the birds and animals—all nature. That has been the dominant influence of his life and career ever since. His record of accomplishment is prodigious and of the greatest importance to every Minnesotan and has had national influence and recognition. He was first elected to the Legislature in 1954. There was a two-year break when he unsuccessfully sought a seat in the Senate. One of his first major projects was a statewide study of water pollution. It focused attention on a major problem that had been ignored. One of its results was the formation of the Lake Superior Sanitary District which led to sewage treatment plants for communities along the St. Louis River, ending a major pollution of Lake Superior. In 1973 he became chair of the House Environment and Natural Resources Committee. Of 346 bills received, 165 were passed by the committee, 128 were approved by the Senate and became law. Some would argue that too much was done too fast and Munger would agree there is always room for review and improvement, but Munger's was a strong voice on issues that needed to be raised. Of all his accomplishments the one he prizes most is the constitutionally provided trust fund to accumulate from lottery and other taxes the income which will provide funding for long-range environmental projects. Munger hopes it will be permitted to grow to a $1 billion fund. Munger's grandfather certainly would be proud of Willard. With profound thanks we wish him a happy 85th birthday.

# Personal Recollections

*Elmer L. Andersen is well known for his love of books and the printed word in any format. He continues to peruse catalogs, sell and buy rare books and donate many to a variety of cultural and educational institutions.*

# Living Out a Fantasy With a Book Catalog

## 1-3-85

Almost everyone needs some escape or diversion from the stressful activities, or boring inadequacies, of everyday life. Most have a variety, ranging from spectator to participant, and covering a wide range of activities. Attending a wrestling match or other athletic contest is a way for many to let off steam, work off animosities or experience exhilarating thrills.

Some 90,000 people felt the Prince concerts their preferred outlet last week and many more, in considerable contrast, find religious experience the most satisfying. Some can curl up with a book and achieve vicarious fulfillment.

One of my particular joys is living out a fantasy with a book catalog. When most of us think of books we think of libraries and a wonderful source they are. If one wants to own a book there are many bookstores ready to accommodate. If that is too expensive a route to go, there are the second hand book stores, the Goodwill and Salvation Army outlets, and the benefit book sales where "next to new" books are sold at bargain prices.

Not so well known are the rare book dealers and auction houses which deal with first editions and early printings of great works. It is a surprise to many to learn that books printed four and five hundred years ago are still on the market and that copies appear for sale that may have only been issued in numbers of 200 or less. Some command high prices, others are surprisingly reasonable and tastes and fads can change affecting market values.

My fantasy is to take a catalog from one of the scholarly rare book dealers which will contain illustrated descriptions of important works, dream how wonderful it would be to select and order what I would like to own—study the catalog, encircling the numbered items that particularly appeal to me and after an hour or so of this distracting and relaxing fun, put the catalog aside, and get back to reality.

Actually my long time love of fine books leads me to order some, at least to assuage my conscience with the dealers who give me so much enjoyment.

A case in point is the catalog of a Boston book dealer which arrived this week. My interest was aroused by the first paragraph of the dealer's statement on the inside front cover when he said many of the books were from the Robert Hoe library which was disbursed in 1911 and had been in one family ever since. Hoe was the greatest book collector of the 19th century and was known to buy only books in the finest condition and of the greatest significance.

Printing from movable type is generally credited to Gutenberg and dated in the 1550s. His great work was the *Gutenberg Bible*. The last copy sold brought $5 and ½ million. The catalog at hand had a copy of the *Nuremberg Chronicle*, printed by Anton Koberger in 1493 (yes, one year after Columbus) which purported to be the whole history of the world from the creation down to the then present and which the catalog claims as "the most famous and most lavish 15th Century book." Are you ready? The price is only $13,000.

Maybe you'd rather dream of diamonds and furs, but doesn't that excite you a little? Another prize, once owned by the Duke of Palma is number 108—the *Historia Naturalis of Plinus Secundus*—published in 1476—all that was known of natural science at that time. Beautifully bound in full leather, richly illustrated, and in incredibly fresh condition for the paper was hand made and all rag. To read it you would need to learn Latin but even without Latin you can appreciate the heritage of that volume of knowledge and that artifact more than 500 years old and imagine its journeys through the centuries. Price—$7000.

But even dreams can come at lower prices. For only $200 (less than eight tickets for one evening's entertainment at a Prince concert) item 67 offers a 13 volume set of the complete works of Oliver Wendell Holmes which can amuse, inspire and exalt you for a life time. The volumes are bound in three-quarter tan polished calf, in excellent condition although published in 1895. It is the quality Houghton Mifflin Riverside Edition. Oh, there are many more, but I've gone on much too long, the holidays have passed, it's time to get back to reality but even in writing of it I feel refreshed. I wish you a Happy New Year—and if you want to give it a special verve—get hooked on books.

## *Thursday, July 23, 1987—*
## *A Date To Remember*

### 7-30-87

The heaviest rainfall in Minnesota history, tornadoes in a devilish dance over the metro area, and the only summertime closing of the airport. Up to 10 inches of rain in four hours at some points, at least four inches throughout the area caused flooding of streets and highways and wreaked havoc in many a home and business. It was a dreadful night and we won't soon forget where we were.

Our son Julian, his wife Jamie, and two sons, Nathan four and Benjamin two, were on their way home to Seattle from a trip to

Scotland and changed planes in Minneapolis. They were due in at 5:50 P.M., arrived a little late and we were there to meet them. After visiting for about an hour their continuing flight was called, we said our farewells and they boarded.

Our route home was north on Cleveland Ave. The sky was threatening and the radio reported a severe thunderstorm approaching. In a few minutes came the tornado warning and report of the touchdown in Maple Grove. People were urged to take cover. We pulled over at a small restaurant, went in and then came the downpour. The sky turned darker and darker until it was really black.

After about an hour, although it was still raining the sky seemed to be lightening so we thought we might progress home. We had not driven very far when another wave of exceedingly heavy rain came making driving almost impossible. We went through one intersection flood on Cleveland in fear we might stall. We encountered another at University and Hampden and as we went through it our hazard lights suddenly came on, but the car didn't stall.

We crawled along to County Road B and went over to Fairview and turned north again. A car was blocking the underpass at Highway 36 and the occupant waved people away. We decided we would have to go through the obstacle course of construction work at Snelling and B and luckily made it through without incident. We were now close to home and the rain abated so we were able to get out of the car and in the house readily. I couldn't get the hazard lights to go off, decided there was a short and I would just have to leave it.

To relax we decided to have some coffee, crackers and the Orkney Island cheese the travelers brought us. Afterwards I checked the phone messages and there was one from our son Tony who was pinned down at the Holiday Inn in St. Louis Park and hoped we were OK. We called back and said that a quick check of our basement and the yard indicated we had escaped damage although a little water had seeped into the basement.

It was now after eleven, we were weary and went to bed. All along we were grateful that our son and his family had managed to get off to Seattle before the storm broke.

At seven Friday morning Julian was on the phone, not from Seattle, but from the airport! The plane had taxied into position but the storm broke before they could get off, pilots decided to wait out the storm but after two hours canceled the flight; shortly after that the airport was closed. There was a rumor that lightning had struck the tower and knocked out the radar system.

There was nothing for stranded passengers to do but sleep in the chairs or on the floor and wait for later planes. A Seattle plane was scheduled for 9:45 A.M. Friday which our group boarded promptly. It became delayed and it was two hours later before it took off. They finally did reach Seattle, exhausted but safe.

Two people died in the storm, some were injured, homes were destroyed, basement walls collapsed, power outages were common, but all in all it was remarkable that more tragedies did not occur. Think what could have happened the night before when the Aquatennial torchlight parade and a Twins game brought 140,000 people into the Minneapolis downtown area. Even those who lost the most were expressing thanks that it was not worse.

Yes, Thursday July 23, 1987 will be a date to remember and it will take some time for the effects to be absorbed and for life to move on.

# The Friendship Of Books

A few days ago the publishing firm of R. R. Bowker announced the publication of the latest edition of *Books in Print*, a compilation of all the books in the United States still available from the original publisher. The total is the most ever, 800,000 volumes. That's new books, in addition there are additional thousands of books, now out of print but available from the used and rare book dealers of our country. And that's just our country. In addition are all the countries of the world and their publications, new in print, and used and rare. The total number of books available worldwide is colossal.

There are many important influences and impacts parents can have on children. Surely one of the most important is to instill a love of reading and books. It begins with reading to them. Who cannot recall those wonderful hours when mother or dad would read a favorite story over and over until we knew it word for word. No child should be denied that evening story hour.

Along with that is developing the desire to have books of one's own. Books and authors become special friends. Always there when you want them, demanding nothing, but offering the best in knowledge, thought and inspiration that has accumulated throughout all time. Modern technology of printing and illustration produces volumes of incredible beauty, but sometimes the simple worn and tattered loved old volume means the most.

Many have expressed why books mean so much to them. One who said it well a great many years ago was Philip De Bury who wrote: "Books are masters who correct our ignorance without putting it to shame. They instruct us without rods and ferules, without hard words and anger, without clothes or money. If you approach them, they are not asleep; if investigating, you interrogate them, they conceal nothing; if you mistake them, they never grumble; if you are ignorant, they cannot laugh at you. They are the most patient and gentle of our teachers, and the most to be cherished."

A family that reads books, loves books, owns books has a window on the world with a special view, and members with a broadened horizon.

## *Living With Older People*
### 3-16-89

Not only are more people living longer but older citizens are now the fastest growing segment of the population. Many are remarkably self sufficient. Men and women well into their 80s and even past 90 take care of themselves and participate in community affairs. Some have limited incomes but many are quite well to do and have a wealth of experience to share.

There are some common characteristics among the older that are well to recognize by those who would like to associate with them economically, socially or out of family loyalty. First of all, they like to be independent and although there may be diminution of faculties they are happy to be getting along as well as they do. They welcome assistance when it is needed but don't liked to be fussed over or intruded upon when they don't need help.

One common trait is the diminution of power of one or more

faculties. Eyesight may be first and fine print a frustration. If you want your ad or directions read by them, use good size type. Hearing can be a problem. Don't shout at them, particularly if they are wearing a hearing aid. With the aid of that remarkable device they may be hearing better than you are. It does help to talk directly to an older person rather than with your back to them as you get something from the shelf. Public speakers, pastors, lecturers should be urged to maintain a minimum volume that reaches all parts of the room where they are speaking. It is incredible how many speakers let their voices trail off to nothing and then wonder why listeners have blank expressions.

Eating can be something of a problem, partly because of the use of dentures or due to health problems. It is probably considerate to ask older guests in advance of an event if what you are planning to serve presents any problem and if something else would be more appropriate.

Include them. Some afflictions such as Parkinson's disease and Alzheimer's can be tragically limiting but it is amazing the spirit that is shown by handicapped people in their desire to be included and continue active. Ideally the special allowances are made as inconspicuously as possible so the older person feels comfortable and an active part of the group.

People who have been helpful and participating in their younger years like to continue that role as much as they can so it is considerate to find ways they can still be justified in feeling they are contributing and not be depressed by "uselessness."

Family life can be enriched by the elderly and they can be a lasting influence on the very young. Attitude has much to do with health in the later years. With a fair degree of good health and understanding and loving family and friends nearby there can be rich dividends for all in a beautiful sunset of life.

# Serving On Jury Duty

## 11-18-89

For the third time in my life I was called for jury duty recently and reported last week Monday. It is always an interesting experience, however inconveniently it may come. Because I live in Ramsey County I reported to the 8th floor jury assembly room in the city hall building in downtown St. Paul. I had not been in the building for sometime and looked forward to seeing the Karl Milles "God of Peace" statue again.

If you have never seen it let me tell you a little about it. The court house was built in the late 1920s and the commission in charge thought it should contain a memorial to veterans of our wars and the architects designed a beautiful hall as the setting for an appropriate sculpture. Internationally famous Swedish sculptor Karl Milles presented the concept of a "God of Peace" which was chosen. Native Americans are seated around a fire smoking their peace pipes. As the smoke arises a figure towering Native American figure emerges, smoking a giant peace pipe. There is the "God of Peace."

The statue is made of a cream colored Mexican onyx, rises massively about thirty feet and is most impressive. It is mounted on a pedestal which moves from side to side so that every time you enter you get a somewhat different perspective. The whole project was a noble concept, created by one of the worlds great sculptors and presented so beautifully that every visit is a moving experience.

## Back To The Jury Assembly Room

Jurors are chosen by lot from the entire district and represent an interesting cross section of the people. As jury panels are needed for cases to be tried names are drawn from the tumbler, 24 or so for criminal cases, about a dozen for civil or misdemeanor cases. For the latter the jury finally selected will be six with one sitting in, in reserve, and for the criminal cases 12, again with an additional reserve.

Jury duty now is limited to one week service for which one is paid $15 a day plus mileage. Employers are required not to deduct wages for jury duty. Service can extend beyond a week if one is chosen on a case that is not settled within the term. That was what happened to me; I was drawn on a panel and then selected for a case that is running beyond the stipulated week.

When seated in the jury box the jurors rise to be sworn in and then receive instructions from the judge, primarily not to discuss the case being heard with each other or anyone else until in the jury room for decision. Cases always seem to proceed slowly but attorneys for both sides are anxious that all relevant evidence is presented.

## Trial By Jury A Precious Right

As I sat and listened for the past week I was reminded what a privilege it is to live in a country where the trial by jury is preserved and carefully protected. Any person can bring a matter before the court, and if hailed into court on an alleged violation can request trial before a jury of fellow citizens. Results are not always to the complete satisfaction of everyone but it is a privilege to have and a basic responsibility of citizenship to be ready to serve when called.

# A Letter That Warms My Heart

### 12-28-89

Someone named Francesco Petrarca wrote a letter to a friend back in 1346, a portion of which a book dealer used as a preface to a catalog. It warms my heart for I know the affliction:

"Divine favour has freed me from most human passions, but one insatiable lust remains which hitherto I have been neither able nor willing to master. I cannot get enough books. Perhaps I already have more than I need, but it is with books as it is with other things: success in acquisition spurs the desire to find still more. Books, indeed, have a special charm. Gold, silver, gems, purple raiment, a house of marble, a well-tilled field, paintings, a steed with splendid trappings: things such as these give us only a silent and superficial pleasure. Books delight us profoundly, they speak to us, they give us good counsel, they enter into an intimate companionship with us."

♣ ♣♣ ♣

# Brighten The Corner Where You Are!

### 4-3-93

As a child I attended a little Sunday School run by the evangelistic Nazarene Church. It was a happy place with a song book of peppy tunes. I still remember one, "Brighten the Corner Where You Are." It may sound like a corny title to some, but it has a message.

There are some people who are disappointed in the job they have, their lot in life, or any of several other factors affecting them—and let it show. They are confident they could and would do so well if a break came their way. Because of their attitude and performance the "breaks" are discouraged from coming.

There are other people I have known who are smiling, cheery, optimistic, wherever they are. Isn't it a treat when you have a sales clerk who is energetic, interested in you and what you are trying to buy, and makes it a pleasant experience for you? A person's attitude, demeanor, expression, and manners, make a big difference in how other people react to them, and make a big difference in how they feel about themselves.

If people work only at the level of the job they have, they will probably stay there. It is reaching out in enthusiasm, energy, initiative, and thoughtfulness, beyond the requirements of the job you have that projects you into promotion and growth.

If there is one thing I have learned about people and their accomplishments, it is not the difference in people's endowment or ability that makes the difference in their accomplishment and growth but what they do with what they have. Record books are filled with the stories of people who overcame every kind of difficulty, disadvantage, handicap or disability, and went on to build useful, successful happy lives. One common characteristic is a personality reflecting joy, enthusiasm, love, caring, helping others, and going that extra mile. People who brighten the corner where they are tend to move into larger space.

# Traveling A Great Deal In Minnesota

### 6-24-93

It was said of Henry David Thoreau that "he traveled a great deal around Walden Pond." His description of his simple life at Walden, near Concord, Mass., and his observations and reflections on nature and life became world classics.

There never was a better time for world travel from the standpoint of ease and economy of air travel to all parts of the world. There is an appeal to getting a glimpse of life and culture in other nations. There is also something to be said for focusing more intensively on life close to home that can frequently go undiscovered by nearby residents.

Very few people could claim to have visited and learned about all parts of Minnesota in depth and understanding. Ours is a remarkable state in the diversity of its geology, topography, natural resources, human history and cultural opportunities. The North Shore of Lake Superior is one such nearly unique area. It has a geological history that goes back a billion years with features found only in one other place on earth—Iceland. The human history of the early explorers, fur traders, lumberjacks, generations of fisher folk, writers, naturalists, native Americans, all make it a fascinating area for visit and study—to say nothing of the bracing air, the magnificence of Lake Superior, the tree lined roads and highways, beautiful flora and fauna and the unexplainable spell it casts on all who come to know it.

There's the iron range, the boundary waters canoe country, Voyageurs National Park, the singular beauty of the endless fertile fields of northwestern Minnesota, and the bird havens of the Lake Traverse area in far western Minnesota. Central Minnesota has marvelous lakes, the Hill Monastic Manuscript Library, south-western Minnesota the Pipestone National Monument and famous Hiawatha Pageant. In southern Minnesota there are rivers, historic monuments, and notable industries. Some of the most beautiful scenery is in the wooded hills of southeastern Minnesota bordering on the Mississippi. The historic Mayo Clinic at Rochester, the fascination of Lake Pepin at Lake City are intriguing, The Metropolitan area itself could take years of exploring and enjoying—not only museums, theaters, historic homes, colleges, concerts, sports, restaurants, but beautiful parks and famous natural wonders such as Minnehaha Falls.

Everywhere there are excellent facilities. Many organizations offer guided tours for those who prefer that to independent adventure. Hunting and fishing in Minnesota occupies many people with just that one aspect of life here. This is a great time to shut off the TV, pack up and go and tell your friends, "We're going to do a lot of traveling around Minnesota". What a treat for the kids to go somewhere new every weekend, with planning and reading preparation in between. Have fun!

♦♣♠♦

# The Importance Of Lifetime Learning
### 8-23-93

This 20th Century has seen the greatest explosion of new knowledge in all history. Every facet of human life, whether health, employment, home conveniences, agricultural, manufacturing and every other technology, exploration, archeology, even religion have been impacted and in many cases vastly changed.

It should be obvious that if we are going to even remotely keep pace with what is going on in the world we need to be studying and learning all the time. Similarly if we are going to do our present jobs better and prepare for greater opportunity we must prepare and advance in our knowledge, skills and productivity. Some people, very early, feel they are too old to do serious study in school or even on their own. The fact is that the older we are the more obsolete much of our training and knowledge has become and all the more reason to seek to improve.

A life of learning is satisfying and rewarding. To make a habit of reading serious books, taking courses in person, by correspondence or even by video—any way whatever—enriches life. It puts one in touch with interesting people who are also seeking to improve. It takes some effort to make learning a habit, a regular and priority part of life, but once established, like any other habit, is easy to maintain.

Many middle aged and older people entered the job market, for example, before computers were strongly entrenched and have never become computer literate. Some executives can have computers in their organization but not be able to operate one. It is tremendously important that everyone who expects to be current and competitive in the job market, no matter what their job, should become computer literate. Furthermore, by making a computer a part of one's personal tools, equipped with a modem, a person can tap into data banks and information sources of incredible extent and variety.

This is no time to live a restricted, narrowly defined life. Everyone of us now relates very directly to everyone else on earth. If we don't apply ourselves, the world will go right by us. If we are alert, interested, curious and involved in one way or another with life-time learning we will understand developments better and be a positive force for ourselves and others, wherever we are.

♣ 🌲🌲 ♣

## *Princeton To Dedicate New Library*

9-14-95

With justifiable civic pride Princeton will dedicate its splendid new library next week Saturday, the 23rd. The building will be open for the occasion at 1 P.M., the program is scheduled for 2 o'-clock, in the Community Room, with refreshments to follow. Robert Boese, Librarian of the East Central Regional library at Cambridge, will be a principal speaker.

Already in use, appropriateness describes the new addition to Princeton's facilities and resources. Beautifully situated on the Rum River, one block from the center of the community, it is skillfully designed by architects Mulfinger, Susanka and Mahady to accommodate the expanding services of a modern community library. Networking makes vast resources available to every user and electronic communication opens the window to the entire world. Modern technology and equipment provide diverse com-munication and learning opportunities.

For thousands of years libraries have been the measure of a so-ciety's or community's level of culture and development. The Co-lumbia Encyclopedia identifies the earliest library as a collection of clay tablets in Babylonia in the 21st Century B.C. Other early li-

88

braries were the Babylonia library in Nineveh, and the sacred library in the Temple at Jerusalem. In 330 B.C. the first public library was established in Greece to preserve accurate copies of the work of the great Greek dramatists. The most famous libraries of antiquity were in Alexandria, Egypt, and Pergamum, an ancient city of Asia Minor, now in Turkey.

Some of the earliest writings were on scrolls and for centuries books were manuscript copies, prepared by monks in monasteries who might work for years on one copy of a beautifully illuminated precious work. In more recent years the Vatican library in Rome is an incredible repository of important work, as is the Library of the British Museum and our own Library of Congress. Libraries have been important in the spread of learning and the development of civilization. The love of learning enriches life, and lifetime learning becomes a necessity as the rapid increase of new knowledge and technology requires continual growth in a person's ability to be a viable member of modern society. Princeton's new library will be a significant force in the community for generations.

*Political Parties, Candidates, Campaigns,*
*Elections and Endorsements*

# Robert Short:
## Campaign Funds Out At Interest

### 10-19-78

U.S. Senate candidate Robert Short is not only spending more money than any previous candidate for Minnesota public office, but expects to get it back, plus interest. In a surprise revelation in his campaign expenditure report to state and federal election officials it was disclosed that the Short-advanced campaign funds, at the million mark as of Sept. 30th, had not been contributed to Short's volunteer committee but loaned, with interest levied at 2 percent a quarter or 8 percent per year. If he is elected, are there to be fund-raising receptions, off the record of course, "to honor the new senator" so that all interested in gaining favor with him can come in with their contributions that will wind up in his pocket "to repay loans to the volunteer committee?" Has he no principles whatever? How else would the loan be repaid? Is there some kind of tax loophole that would permit charging off the loan as a "bad debt" and thus making it a deductible item in figuring income tax? If this is possible it would be a cute way of recovering most of the money at the expense of the unsuspecting taxpayer. Whatever the method of recovery it now appears that Short is not spending "my own hard earned money" but is simply making another investment which he expects to more than fully recover, even though his campaign manager says lamely that Short does not expect to "get" much of it back. If he expects or wishes little or no repayment, why handle it as a loan? Another interesting campaign committee report disclosure was that a group which issued material attacking Fraser during the primary with which Short, apparently, did not want to be publicly identified, and which filed campaign reports too late to be released before the primary election, was almost entirely financed with Short money—$40,000 out of $40,035 spent.

We cannot believe that Minnesotans are going to vote to send a man to the U.S. Senate who is so unrepresentative of the basic honesty, decency, morality and forthrightness of the people of our state.

★🌲🌲★

# A Future For Sen. Durenberger
## 7–26–90

In appraising what attitude to take toward Sen. David Durenberger, now that the Senate Ethics Committee has made its recommendation, the decision should center around what is best for Minnesota and the country not what is appropriate "punishment" for him. To be called before the Senate for "denouncement" is an ordeal. In the committees judgment he "knowingly and willfully" broke rules and violated regulations in his effort to improve his financial situation. Has he a viable future as a Senator?

We continue to feel that he should not resign. Certain facts weigh heavily with us. At no time has there been any evidence that he violated his public trust on public issues coming before him for decision. His record now, as it has been for 30 years, is one of hard work and devotion to the public interest. People who follow legislative matters know that.

Can he be effective? At the height of the investigations he was named to the conference committee on the Clean Air Act and also to the conference committee on the Persons With Disabilities Act—two of the most important projects of the session, on both of which he played key roles. There is no question his legislative ability and influence is recognized and is unimpaired.

He has seniority, important committee assignments and is strongly positioned to be influential on health care, environmental, budget and other crucial matters coming before the Senate. Can the *Star Tribune* or any others calling for his resignation make any case that a new appointee could be as effective? Durenberger made serious mistakes, there is no doubt about that. We believe it is in our own best interest that he continue to demonstrate his legislative powers and show that he has learned a personal lesson, at great cost to himself and his family, friends, supporters and constituents, from which he can emerge as a wiser, more careful and still useful United States Senator for Minnesota and the nation.

## *Oh For A Suburban Caucus!*

### 10-4-90

Preliminary reports of the 1990 census indicate that the central cities of St. Paul and Minneapolis are barely holding the population of 10 years ago but that the suburbs have continued to grow, now reaching a point of nearly double the population of St. Paul and Minneapolis. If you add the secondary levels of suburbs just outside the metro area the domination of the suburbs becomes greater. This means that after the reapportionment the position of the suburbs and outer suburbs in the legislature will be substantially enhanced.

The trouble is the suburbs have never been able to put together a united caucus. Edina finds it hard to relate to Roseville needs, and S. St. Paul is a long way from Anoka, legislatively. In contrast, Hennepin County legislators go into every session with a specific agenda for the city and county, have regular meetings, deploy their members through the legislature as chairpeople of key committees and have influence far beyond their numbers. St. Paul and Ramsey County do the same thing and no group is better organized or fiercer in their struggle for local advantage than the legislators from the Range and Duluth. That's why the rest of the state can frequently get shafted. Ask Bloomington about the loss of the stadium to Minneapolis, or any of the suburban school districts about finance equity. Minneapolis, St. Paul and Duluth school districts receive special aid based on the number of children in school from families receiving Aid to Families with Dependent Children. The formula for qualification is designed to keep out School District 11, Anoka which has a large number of AFDC children.

Someday, somehow the legislators from the suburbs should be brought together to realize that their communities have many mutual problems and that in combination the suburban legislators have a lot of untapped power if they but put it all together.

# The Dangerous Power Of PACs

8-16-90

It was a labor union, wishing to get around the prohibition of using union funds for political contributions, that dreamed up the idea of a Political Action Committee that could raise unlimited amounts of money outside of union dues and distribute them as it chose. Business and other special interest groups were not slow to pick up on the idea and by 1974 there were 608 PACs which raised and contributed $12.5 million in that year's campaigns. The idea has exploded since. In 1988 there were 4828 PACs which raised $151 million.

It would be naive, indeed, not to recognize that this represents political power and influence that imperils if not destroys traditional political loyalties and responsibilities. What are we to think when candidates for national political office in our own state, as well as in many others raise as much as 75% of their campaign funds outside the districts or states they are elected to serve? Where are their loyalties? Whom do they represent?

It gets so bad that in Washington lobbyists of rival special interest groups get together to compromise proposed legislation and present propositions to Congress that can be passed without offending any of the rival groups and thus threatening contributions.

The flow of PAC funds make it difficult to challenge incumbents. In 1988, 90% of PAC money went to the reelection campaigns of incumbents. Democrats received $67.6 million, Republicans $34.6 million, which blasts the idea that Republicans get all the money. Is it any wonder that 96 to 98% of the incumbent members of Congress running for reelection are re-elected? Is it in the national interest to have such a small turnover? Present rules permit retiring members of Congress to retain for personal use any balances in their campaign committee fund. Was it ever intended that members of Congress should build personal fortunes from campaign contributions? Some, such as retiring Bill Frenzel, do not take advantage of such possibilities but dispose of the balance to charitable or worthy political efforts.

Common Cause and some members of Congress have favored campaign finance reform that would bar PACs as well as establish other limits but in the partisan struggle for advantage little gets done. The abuse has reached the stage to justify public outrage and effective reaction. It is unconscionable beyond all toleration.

## *It Was A Remarkable Election*
### 11-15-90

In what is being referred to as "the most bizarre election in Minnesota history," a large turnout of voters last Tuesday elected present State Auditor Arne Carlson, Governor and Carleton College professor Paul Wellstone, United States Senator—both by narrow margins over incumbents Governor Rudy Perpich and U. S. Senator Rudy Boschwitz.

Allegations about the personal life of Republican nominee Jon Grunseth led to his withdrawal and in a tumultuous few days Carlson went from a write in candidate to the official candidate of his party on a last minute specially printed ballot. He will come to the office as particularly well experienced with service as a Minneapolis council member, a legislator and several years as state auditor. He is thought of as representing the more moderate or less conservative wing of the Republican party. He will have the challenge of working with a DFL controlled legislature in handling reapportionment of the state for both legislative and congressional districts, resolving difficult budget, appropriation and tax issues, and quickly selecting a team of administrators and preparing budget recommendations.

Paul Wellstone, with a long record of political interest and activity became a candidate for the Senate when others were shying away from challenging the popular and well funded Rudy Boschwitz. From the beginning Wellstone had absolute confidence in his ability to get the endorsement, nomination and win election. His election is an inspiration to all other potential candidates, proving as it did that conviction and determination coupled with clever commercials and mistakes by his opponent can defeat incumbency, popularity and millions of campaign funds.

Wellstone and Carlson will bring fresh beginnings to Minnesota politics. From a near debacle Minnesota voters proved themselves able to sort out a confused picture and make selective judgments that gained national positive attention.

# McCarthy And Stassen

3-19-92

Some time ago radio and TV stations were required to give equal time to all presidential candidates of the two major parties. That became cumbersome and the electronic media managed to get a provision that the candidates listed by the parties as major candidates would be the only ones considered. Harold Stassen is a candidate on the Republican ticket and former Senator Eugene McCarthy on the Democrat. Because neither was certified by their respective party, they have been ignored.

Both had long and honorable public careers as well as personal lives of integrity and character. Both are intelligent and knowledgeable. Both offer themselves because they feel they have contributions to make and feel a sense of mission and commitment regardless of how the public may view their candidacies and the little likelihood of becoming presidential nominees.

Both are natives of Minnesota of whom the state can be proud. It is to the credit of the state legislature that it has given Stassen an opportunity to speak in the legislative chamber and a similar courtesy is being extended to McCarthy. If people will only listen they will find both of these men offering sensible solutions to national and international problems, several cuts above the talk of candidates more involved in winning elections than seriously facing problems with forthright discussion.

Minnesota's media and organizations should extend every opportunity afforded others to these two native sons so that people remember them when going to vote in Minnesota's presidential primary. A good vote would be a well earned salute to two worthy public servants.

# What Should Republicans Do Now?

## 11-26-92

Minnesota Independent Republicans (a name that came about to help shed an image of too much conservatism) have built such a narrow based one issue party that it requires substantial renovation if it is to survive. It is interesting that Rep. Tim Penny is concerned with the Democrats going too far to the left with Sen. Wellstone's Alliance and the Republicans have gone so far to the right that it leaves the entire middle of the political spectrum without a party.

Minnesota is a progressive state. It has been innovative, experimental and contributing in many fields of education, governance and social service. It has a large segment of independents who gave Perot substantial support in the early stages of his campaign and even as an in and outer he drew many votes in our state. Obviously many were dissatisfied with both parties. Gov. Clinton was elected president with a minority of the popular vote.

It should be a major concern of Gov. Arne Carlson that the party be rebuilt under the broad appeal that characterized its success for many years. It should be evident that the abortion issue is settled for some time to come. Most people do not favor abortions but they don't want laws limiting a woman's choice. That should be clear. It would be more constructive now to put great emphasis on limiting unwanted pregnancies through counseling, education, church and family influence and every other way possible, particularly among the young and unmarried. The second big emphasis should be on prenatal care and guidance so children brought to term have a healthy, happy loving entrance to life. Those who cannot accept that program should stand aside for the great majority who do. The moderates of the Republican party should go into the caucuses and take back the party and return to openness, a welcoming of divergent views, a reconciliation through the convention and platform process and get on to returning Minnesota to leadership in education, health care, economic development, agricultural prosperity, tourism and all the other areas of our diverse society. We are blessed with natural resources and outstanding people. Political leadership is needed, and it will either come from the governor or it will rise up from the ranks. Minnesota Republicanism will not be in the political doldrums very long.

## They Also Serve Who Run And Lose

### 11-11-93

As soon as results are clear, in any election, attention turns to the winners, their plans, their prospects, the keys to the win. We want to offer a salute to the losers who play an important role in our democratic process which should not be overlooked or go unappreciated.

Last Wednesday's elections found many incumbents replaced, in local elections and in state races of national interest. It is a keen disappointment for people who have served, done what they thought was right and yet suffer what appears to be a repudiation and humiliation. It should not be so considered. Today's fiscal and social problems make elective office, at any level, a virtual no-win situation. It is exceedingly hard to find effective and acceptable solutions. Many people have lost confidence in government feeling it costs too much for what it delivers. Winning back that confidence is a major challenge—to the public to take more interest and become better informed—to the candidates to conduct campaigns that are honest in presentations and realistic in what is promised.

Anyone who serves in public office ultimately learns that the main reward is the personal satisfaction of knowing that one was willing to serve, was given the opportunity, and made a contribution to keep democracy working. When relieved by the electorate, he or she can go back to personal concerns. There should be some sense of relief. Later, it may develop that a defeat was a blessing, though not recognized nor appreciated at the time.

Then there are those who decide to give of time and energy to seek public office and are denied. That can be a severe disappointment, also, and a shock to self esteem. The fact is that few candidates win their first attempt at public office. Politics, at any level, is demanding and can certainly be frustrating and discouraging. Everyone can share in the effort to improve the process. Contests are essential to shaping public policy and with contests go personal disappointments. Losers have performed an important service as candidates and are entitled to stand tall, learn from the experience, and try again.

We are blessed to have the freedom of the election process and can be thankful that each election, for offices at all levels, there are people willing to serve. Winning or losing, two additional satisfying dividends of politics and public service are the widening of one's friendships and acquaintances and coming to understand the diversities of our country and how it works. Anyone who participates is, in the broadest sense, a winner.

# Caucus Is Place To Make A Difference

2-10-94

On March 1, in every voting district in the state, the two major parties will hold caucuses to elect delegates to conventions and name district officers. Also resolutions will be offered, endorsing candidates or taking positions on issues of interest. It is the grass roots beginning of the election process. Party platforms and party endorsed candidates all rely on the results of the precinct caucuses.

The parties usually name a convenor of the caucus in advance but an early action is to elect a caucus chair. This quickly determines who has the votes to control the caucus, decide issues and name delegates. Those wishing to have influence must not only attend the caucus but bring enough friends along to organize and control it. Organization is the source of political power. In many voting districts of the state a very few people attending can organize and control. In voting districts in the metro area there can frequently be hotly contesting rival groups that result in 200 or 300 people attending an individual caucus.

Our political process depends upon political power and that power springs from the caucus. Some attenders just like to be in on the process, express views and submit resolutions, without a big effort to take control. To control a caucus takes organization and hard work but it is the route to follow if one wants to make a difference.

In the DFL party there is concern that the party is going too far to the left. In the Independent Republican Party there is concern that the party has gone too far to the right and become a one issue, anti-abortion party and is intolerant of differing views. To bring about change, or to keep the status quo, will require attendance at the caucuses. That's where the decisions will be made that will determine the policies and candidates of the parties for the next two years, except as they are changed in the primary election. Caucus information is available from the party of choice, or in a copy of election laws from the Secretary of State office at the capitol. Political participation is interesting and exciting, and fundamental to the operation of a democracy.

🌲🌲🌲🌲

# Using A Constitutional Convention For Restructuring

## 3-25-93

This session of the legislature has many bills calling for changing governmental organization and process. Some call for a unicameral or one house legislature, limitation of terms, combination of government units, concentration of departments, constitutional amendments with various provisions. Usually the legislature finds it difficult to give governmental reorganization much serious attention, badly as it is needed.

Minnesota is one of very few states that has never had a constitutional convention since the first one. Many states have had more than one convention to periodically review government organization by a specially elected convention of delegates. Many of a state's ablest citizens are willing to contribute time for a one time concentrated effort to better state government.

In the 1940s Gov. Luther Youngdahl appointed a commission under the chairmanship of Sen. Gordon Rosenmeier to study the constitution and make recommendations. In its report the commission suggested calling a constitutional convention to consider updating, housecleaning and modifying the constitution. The League of Women Voters made it a major project but the legislature declined to take the necessary action. It is up to the legislature to submit the question of having a convention to a vote of the people. If the people declare in favor of a convention the legislature provides the rules for electing delegates, after they are chosen and convene, the delegates deliberate and make such changes as they decide upon.

Some objected that the people did not have a chance to pass on the constitution before it became effective so a constitutional amendment was submitted and adopted which provides that the work of the convention will be subject to voter approval before becoming effective. Suggestions for a convention have been periodic over the years.

Now may be a good time to renew efforts as we prepare for a new century and because there is such an accumulation of government situations requiring improvement for greater efficiency and economy. State and local government is weighed down with many costly burdens of faulty organization and process that could be revised in a constitutional convention. The amendment method of providing needed changes is too cumbersome and faulted by the requirement that adoption of a constitutional amendment requires a majority of all voting at the election so those not voting count against a proposal. That is an antiquated provision in itself and hampers progress. We would urge the legislature to submit the question to the voters and give them a chance to decide whether or not they would like to have a constitutional convention.

# Carlson For Governor, Wynia For U.S. Senator

## 11–3–94

Next Wednesday, Nov. 8, is election day. It certainly is to be hoped that a large voter turnout will make the necessary choices. In a time of rapid economic and social change, and particularly in a democracy, it is crucial that citizens take the time and effort to be informed and participate in the election process. Voters can chose from the entire ballot in the final election, it is not necessary to vote a "straight ticket." Many Minnesotans consider themselves independent so split tickets are more the rule than the exception.

In the September primary voters made it clear they wanted no part of the Quist ideology. Gov. Arne Carlson has had a productive administration, solved difficult financial problems, has made progress in health care extension and welfare reform, has an administration team in place. He has combined sound governmental judgment with political skill. His reelection will reassure those who have praised the state for effective management. A strong vote of confidence will aid Carlson in his working relationships with the legislature.

State Senator John Marty has drawn attention to greater emphasis on education, particularly higher education, crime prevention through early attention versus emphasis on punishment and prisons. He remains in his legislative office and will continue to have an opportunity to express his viewpoints and pursue his objectives. It would not be sensible to turn the governorship over to him at this time.

We reaffirm our endorsement of Ann Wynia for the United States Senate. Because your publisher is basically a Republican some express surprise and disappointment that a DFL candidate is endorsed. It is not the first time and should at least testify to our efforts to be bipartisan, fair and objective in the conduct of this newspaper. We believe that anyone who knew both of the candidates personally and studied their records would readily conclude that Minnesota would be much better represented and served by Ann Wynia. Having worked under a state constitution that requires a balanced budget she can be expected to have concern about deficits and rising debt.

A vote for Gov. Arne Carlson to continue as governor and Ann Wynia to be Minnesota's first elected woman United States Senator will be a proud vote.

DISCLAIMER—*Publisher and Chairman Elmer L. Andersen is nominally a Republican but is currently dissatisfied with the posture of the Minnesota Republican party and the leadership of Robertson, Falwell and Buchanan nationally. He appears as Honorary Chair of the Dyrstad for U.S. Senate effort and on the advisory committee of Natalie Haas Steffen for 6th District Congress. He strongly supports Gov. Arne H. Carlson for reelection. He has worked with and supported DFLers. Political persuasion is not a condition of employment at ECM, for editors or others. Editorials are intended to stimulate discussion and participation and columns are open for readers' views.*

# Gov. Carlson Gets A Triple A Rating

5-9-96

When Gov. Arne Carlson first took office in January 1991, his immediate and main challenge was fiscal. Expenditure commitments had been previously made that were hundreds of millions—by some estimates 2 billion—in excess of anticipated revenues. Tax increases to cover would be impossible and he had run on a no-tax increase commitment. The situation was serious enough to catch outside attention and lead companies in the business of rating state securities for the information of investors to lower their rating on Minnesota bonds, thus expressing concern about Minnesota finances and the state's ability to meet all its obligations. There were difficulties getting a stable staff put together, there were a host of social problems needing attention, there were difficulties getting a working arrangement between the DFL Legislature and the new Republican governor following the record tenure of his DFL predecessor. But with his head down, football style, and his traveling legs churning, he tore into the main challenge and gradually brought the people of the state around to his view and in 1994 won a strong reelection despite not being endorsed by his own party.

With stubborn tenacity, a record use of the veto, and with support from legislators of both parties, he prevailed and converted looming deficits into cash surpluses. Last week Moody's, a leading rater of state securities, gave Minnesota securities its top Triple A rating. It was a Triple A rating for the governor as well. Knowing the fiscal challenge had been met, Carlson had already focused with intensity on another problem of great concern to him, the plight of children in our state, the incidence of poverty, neglect, abuse, failure in school, teenage pregnancy, drug addiction, crime—a frightening and devastating litany and a most serious threat to the society's future. Programs to address these problems and needs were scattered throughout state government. Carlson led the effort to bring them together in one department now called the Department of Children, Families and Learning. The former Department of Education is the largest component. Bringing all the agencies that serve children together for efficiency, economy and impact was not unlike a concept Sen. Jerome Hughes proposed several years ago. Last week Carlson emphasized that his focus will be on children rather than structure or process. If he can be as successful in redeeming the lives of children and youth as he has been in redeeming the state's credit rating, it will add much to the record of his administration.

⁂

## Big Business Could Use Its Power Better

### 10-17-96

Through the millions of dollars of political action committee contributions and the maintenance of thousands of lobbyists in Washington, big business, generally identified as firms listed on the stock exchanges, wield tremendous influence on Congress. It has been evident in the actions of both major parties for the past 20 years. It reached a culmination in 1994 with the election of a Republican Congress and the emergence of Rep. Newt Gingrich as Speaker of the House.

Far from becoming the hero of a new day, Gingrich is the least-popular political figure in the country. Bob Dole's ties with him is the reason many people give for favoring Clinton over Dole in the presidential race. What went wrong for the Republicans? There were specific mistakes but, generally speaking, a too-narrowly business-oriented program instead of one that reached more people directly. One major mistake was the proposal to cut the capital gains tax and at the same time resist an increase in the minimum wage. Although business could argue that the best way to increase jobs and wages is to stimulate investment with the capital gains cut, it didn't sell as well as the comment, a tax cut for the rich and no break for the little guy. Another was the act of Congress to shut off funds for the government in order to bring the president to heel. It shocked and outraged the country to see the length Gingrich and Company were willing to go to impose their will on the nation. The intense effort of Senator Al D'Amato to discredit the President and First Lady simply did not catch on.

If big business, with all the influence, wants to win the political confidence of the nation, it must suggest some sacrifice for itself in seeking to balance the budget and reduce the debt. To put the burden of cuts on the poorest people among us is not the way. Business knows there are thousands of special provisions that favor certain industries and even individual companies that could stand review and reduction. To make depreciation schedules more realistic could increase federal revenues by billions. Leaders of American industry are, for the most part, able, enlightened and socially conscious individuals. The lobbyists who represent them think they best serve their principals by getting all they can and ignoring others. The principals need to exert more control.

# Public Policy, Issues Facing Minnesota, The Nation And The World

*In an editorial on June 28, 1994, Elmer L. Andersen wrote: "Each week I write editorials. They are designed to provide information and stimulate thought and activity. There is bound to be some disagreement and critics are encouraged to write letters to the paper for publication. It is always interesting to read critical letters. If the person attacks the writer with whom he or she disagrees, that is not nearly as effective as civilly disagreeing with the opinions or interpretations with their own ideas. If you have ideas for editorials I would be glad to have them. If you have opinions on the editorials that you do not wish to publish I would be glad to have them. Freedom is what our country is all about and the ability to dis-agree without being disagreeable is one of the best characteristics of an American. On the 4th of July, and at every other time, we should be appreciative of our country and seek to make it a better place for everyone."*

*The subject commanding the most editorials written by Elmer L. Andersen over 20 years are myriad issues—local, state, national and global—confronting the human race as it verges on the 21st century. What follows is a selection of such issues examined by the author in his weekly newspapers.*

# MINNESOTA

## Keep U Athletics On Campus

### 2-18-90

In the flurry of discussion about the pros and cons of a new athletic arena on the campus of the University of Minnesota little has been said about the best interest of the students. The discussion has centered around the income that would be generated for downtown St. Paul if U hockey and basketball were there instead of on campus.

It is a fact that since University football went to the Dome, student attendance has fallen. It is hard to maintain student enthusiasm when the athletic games become a downtown commercial activity. One thing that is needed for the good health of student athletics is decommercialization and that is more easily accomplished if the athletic programs are kept on campus.

🌲🌲🌲

## In The Spirit Of Horace Mann

### 2-21-91

Horace Mann, who lived 1796 to 1859, was more responsible than any other one person for the establishing of the Massachusetts State Board of Education in 1837 and through it the development of free public education in his home state and the rest of the nation. He called education "the great equalizer of the conditions of men" and "the balance wheel of the social machinery." Public education broadly available is generally considered the most important factor in generating the economic growth and world ascendancy of the United States.

Minnesota needs leadership in the spirit of Horace Mann to revolutionize our current thinking and place higher education in the position it must be if our people are to have to have a decent place in the world of the 21st century. In the February issue of the *Atlantic Magazine* Robert B. Reich, Harvard professor of political economy, outlines in depth a present world economy in which "the true sources of national wealth are the accrued skills of the work force and the quality of the social and material infrastructure supporting them." Few would question the thesis. If it be true, than the most important thing a state or society can do is develop the talents and skills of its people. The standards of education now current are insufficient for today's world. We need a vision and commitment relative to our day as Horace Mann's was to his—an extension of free education to the full development of every person's talent and ability to provide our future society with its most important asset—a fully developed citizenry for leadership in research, development, and every phase of human activity. We should shed the idea that higher education mainly benefits the person who acquires it and therefore he or she should contribute substantially to its cost through tuition. That idea is obsolete and is making education selective, for those who can afford it and denying our society the potential contributions of those who miss a full educational opportunity.

As part of bold education reform we need to upgrade high school curricula to include math, physics, chemistry, and other solid subjects throughout the four year high school term—at least that should be the requirement for college preparation. We need to lengthen the school day and the school year. We need to give public concern and attention to the health and development of children from conception to school age to minimize the occurrence of impaired or high risk children. We need to lift our concept substantially of what is in the public interest and a matter for public concern and support.

Nothing proposed here would be more revolutionary or require greater relative investment and sacrifice than did Horace Mann's proposals in the early 19th century. A similar vision applied to today's challenges could be expected to bring a societal return comparable to that which came with the introduction of public education. A clear look at the present world situation, a vision of the role Minnesota could play, and a public will to lead the way is the pressing need and tremendous opportunity.

🌲🌳🌲

## Providing Jobs for Rural America
### 9-23-93

Currently, as many times in the past, there is a push to "reinvent" or reform government. There is a way, using modern technology, where federal costs could be reduced and vitality restored to rural America.

Through the marvels of electronic communication offices can be anywhere. It is no longer necessary to accumulate huge offices

in central cities that generate highway problems, urban congestion, social dislocations and all that goes with overcrowding.
Commercial firms are already making use of the opportunities. If
a Minnesotan calls the local Greyhound Lines 800 number for
schedule information for service from St. Paul to Duluth, someone answers from goodness knows where and asks, What state is
Duluth in? If you call Western Union seeking to send a cable to
England, someone in Missouri will answer the St. Paul number
you dial. Calls to a travel agency in Philadelphia wind up in Lin-
ton, North Dakota which prospers as a result.

The eastern seaboard of our country is an area of enormous
congestion and urban problems. Federal government agencies
could ease much of that by moving millions of jobs to rural America. The population would be spread out, pollution would be reduced, people would live in cleaner and better circumstances, federal distribution of expenditures would be equalized, and costs
would be reduced.

It is a radical suggestion but one not without merit worth consideration. In the enormous process of redistribution of jobs as a
part of reforming government there could be a reexamination of
much of what we do. For example, does it make sense to maintain
the hundreds of millions of individual records necessary to person-
alize Social Security payments? Why not a simple guaranteed minimum income at retirement and the present employee/employer
payroll tax financing it? Administration costs would be greatly reduced and people of higher income eliminated from the benefit.
That oversimplifies the change but it demonstrates how we could
simplify governmental operations as we redistribute jobs. The only
reason for drifting along in old costly patterns is the unwillingness
of the people to become more demanding of reform in the public
interest.

# Is It A Handicap To Be Gifted?

## 10-14-93

In an early Minnesota legislative study of problems of so-called handicapped children, which led to a statewide system of special education, one of the first things the participants learned was better terminology. Children in the study were to be identified as exceptional children, and instead of "handicapped," children with disabilities was the preferred designation.

One of the surprises was to find that gifted and talented children were included in the categories of exceptionality. An exceptional child was defined as one who had one or more conditions that rendered the child incapable of benefiting fully from a normal school situation. Exceptional children required special help to learn, depending on the nature and degree of the disability. At that time gifted and talented children were receiving the least attention of those needing special help.

Was a gifted or talented child to be considered as having a disability? No, but a talented and gifted child, then and now, has characteristics needing special attention. Only then can the gifts and talents be fully developed. Neglected or misunderstood, a gifted and talented child, by racing through course work, can become a behavioral problem in the classroom, or an emotionally and mentally disturbed child personally. With appropriate guidance and teaching the gifted or talented child can go on to live a happy life and make substantial contributions to society.

One of the greatest resistances to adequate attention to the gifted and talented is the popular conception that "smart kids can make it on their own" and don't need special attention. Another is failure of parents and teachers to recognize gifted and talented children and see to it that they receive the attention needed. Progress has been slow but fairly steady and there are now local and national organizations of parents and professionals working to recognize and work with children with special gifts as we do with children with disabilities.

A significant advance was made in Minnesota by the 1993 legislative session, in the omnibus K–12 education bill with a provision for staff development funding in school districts where gifted and talented students are identified and challenged with appropriate programs. Parents who have reason to feel one or more of their children have special gifts, whether academic, mechanical, or performing (art, music, drama, athletic) should associate with an interest group and encourage use of the new legislation in the local school district.

Minnesota Council for the Gifted and Talented is a non-profit organization of parents and professionals devoted to promoting better understanding and educational services for gifted and talented children.

🌲🌳🌳🌲

# Education Funding Has Come Full Circle

## 6-2-94

In the early years of this century education and other local government costs were all financed by the property tax. As needs developed and property taxes went up, protests grew. When the depression of the 30s hit property tax default was extensive. Local government was in crisis. It was then that many states introduced the sales tax on the theory that those with money to spend could pay a tax.

In Minnesota. Gov. Floyd B. Olson opted for the income tax with the promise that it would be reserved for education. It was enacted and for 20 years, into the fifties, it was dedicated to education support. During that period Minnesota's splendid system of elementary, secondary and higher education was built. As income tax revenue grew, as well as other costs, particularly welfare, attacks on the income tax dedication grew. A key welfare policy decision was that indigent older people should be provided medical care which was interpreted to include doctor prescribed nursing home care. That spawned the nursing home industry which now receives about 60% of the total welfare budget. Finally, income tax revenue went into the general revenue fund and a heavier school burden fell back on property.

We have now come full circle to another time of property tax crisis and education standards struggling for survival. A logical support for education is income tax because of the direct connection between the two. There is a real question if income tax revenues can be increased enough by economic growth. It would be interesting to have a survey made of the percentage of state and local government expense carried by corporate and other categories of taxpayers now as compared to twenty years ago. If it was disclosed that business or any other segment of the economy was paying less than its previous share, some adjustment would be suggested. The popular political promise of no increase in taxes and reduced spending will not be possible much longer.

Long term health care (nursing home provision) for the indigent, is not the only, but a big factor in Minnesota's increased government cost. People live longer, need nursing home care, which is expensive, and more and more families look to the government to foot the bill. Divesting of assets to qualify for government paid nursing home care has become a legal and financial specialty. It is the enormous budget concern of a national health care system. Few, if any, states provide as does Minnesota.

Our property tax system is at crisis, education support is suffering, government costs are not going to decline nor even be contained unless people are willing to take less in direct payment. Maybe it's time to have a state commission on Tax Reform and Government Benefit Review.

⁂

# Strategy Needed
# For Minnesota Agriculture
## 11-24-94

Recent events in Minnesota agriculture against a report of national trends suggests we need a strategy for this important Minnesota industry. Who can forget the foreclosure sales that put families off their land after a series of drought years led banks to deny further credit. Now we have a banner crop year and prices tumble making it tougher for the survivors to get the return needed to balance the lean years.

Nationally, the alarming news is that the number of farms has fallen to the smallest number since the Civil War. Furthermore, large corporate farms are taking over the industry. In 1992, 2% of the farms, with sales of $500,000 or more produced 46% of the total sales. By contrast 75% of the farms, which had sales under $50,000 produced only 9% of the sales. Despite the obvious need to have larger farms to compete for the sales, 59.1% of farms in the nation are still less than 180 acres. They will be gobbled up by the corporate giants unless something is done about it.

The prospects for U.S. agriculture are promising. We have the technology, the skilled operators, global markets are opening, and standards of living in many areas are rising rapidly. What is needed is marketing assistance and financial availability so our smaller family farms can expand into the $50,000 to $250,000 annual sales range. Nationally this size farm is holding its own against the huge operations and are within the scope of family management with all its advantages for the community and society.

The makeup of the national Congress has become more urbanized and less concerned about continuing farm subsidies for the uneconomic sized farm. Small town and farm survival in Minnesota will depend on a state program that will encourage our farm families to move into economic sized operations. An urban dominated Congress won't provide the leadership required. Agriculture is not mentioned in the Contract With America. Minnesota needs a carefully planned and adequately financed in-depth research program to determine how our trends compare with the national and the means by which a program of financial stability and economic size can be made possible for our fine farm families. It should be a concern of all citizens and a top priority for the legislature when it convenes in January. Rural Minnesota need not go down the drain.

# Minnesota Has A Lot At Stake

## 12-8-94

Minnesotans, particularly those who have lived in other states, have no doubts about the quality of life in our state. Minnesota is attractive in so many ways—its natural resources, its distinctive seasons, its variety of outdoor activities, its educational and cultural opportunities, its systems of public health service, its many civic and social service organizations, its philanthropy, its employment standards, its fine arts and science facilities—there is literally no end. Some of it is aided by state support, much from generous giving by individuals, corporations and foundations, and much of it from federal programs. We have much at stake in any substantial national policy changes or slashing of support under the pretense of "providing more local control."

The most significant result of the November election was the almost complete conversion of southern conservatism to the Republican party. It gave Republicans majority in both houses of Congress. One of the evidences of new southern power was the choice of Sen. Lott of Mississippi to be assistant majority leader of the Senate. That is not a signal that augurs well for Minnesota.

Before the Republicans go too far too fast they should recognize that only 39% of the eligible voters cast ballots at the election so a winning majority was delivered by about 20% of the eligible voters. There are examples, both in 1948 and 1954, of an over eager Republican majority, misreading the mandate and holding their control for only a short time.

Some items in the Contract With America would have almost universal approval, such as subjecting members of Congress to all laws imposed on others.

It is in the area of education, arts, social services, human rights, and research that Minnesotans would be concerned. Sudden, drastic, harsh, mean spirited approaches should be avoided. Ethics and integrity in Washington can be pursued with enthusiastic public support as well as elimination of waste and corruption in the military-industrial complex relationships, and in international arms deals. There is plenty to work on without injuring a splendid relationship between state, federal, and private resources to produce a precious way of life in Minnesota and many other states. We have a lot at stake.

🌲🌲🌲🌲

# Facing Up To A Local International Problem
## 1-19-95

It is hard for many citizens to accept the reality and implications of Native American tribes as sovereign nations, recognized as such through treaties and long established federal law. For years Indians have been ignored and neglected. Now, through their gambling casinos, they are acquiring the means to assert their rights and improve their situation. The result is a growing tension with the most serious implications.

In Mille Lacs County, for example, Ojibwe Chair Marge Anderson is attempting to manage the financial resources of her band for the good of the Ojibwe Community, rather than disbursing funds to individuals. One of her projects is to buy land to add to the Band's holdings and provide for housing expansion and other needs. When she buys land it goes off the tax rolls and the lost revenue must be levied on the remaining property owners. What she is doing is legal and desirable from the Indian standpoint but creates an impossible situation for county taxpayers. What is to be done?

On the matter of fishing and hunting rights, the Band offered an agreement limiting Indian rights as provided in early treaties. Many thought it was fair and should have been accepted. Under pressure from sportsmens' groups the legislature decided to challenge the validity of the treaties in court. The case was lost, though subject to appeal. Extensive treaty rights were upheld and sportsmen are not of a mind to accept the court decision. The prospect is ugly. Come spring, if Indians exercise their rights, particularly as they relate to spearing, violence could occur.

It is simply imperative that Congress solve the problem. It is not possible, with every Indian tribe a separate nation, to have a growing population under separate laws and responsibilities, different from those applying to the rest of the residents of the country. We must become "one nation, indivisible." Heavy handed, one-way solutions won't do. It will take the most sensitive negotiation. Full consideration of Indian rights must be compensated in a fair negotiated way and to their satisfaction. Everyone involved must recognize that the present situation will only get worse. There is no more challenging issue, foreign or domestic, facing our nation.

# Federal Aid Is A Hefty Share Of State Budget

2-16-95

Washington talk of eliminating unfunded federal mandates might suggest that the federal government is dumping problems on the states without funding them. In some cases and to some degree that may be true (no detail is offered) but it should not obscure the fact that federal aid is a hefty share of state revenue. In Minnesota, in 1993, it was 22% or $2.9 billion.

Figures from the Census Bureau indicate that the 1993 Minnesota general revenue of $13.4 billion, major sources were sales taxes, 27%, income tax 25%, federal aid 22%, charges 9%, other taxes 9%. Not many people would estimate that federal aid was that close to our own income and sales tax revenue.

The whole subject of federal and state relationships is highly complicated and should be examined in detail and carefully, not made the subject of simplistic slogans. Some federal mandates are intended to establish national uniformity, as in education, so children are treated equally throughout the country. We have moved away from the right of a state to keep a problem at home and do nothing about it. With an increasingly diverse population we must be ever more sensitive to any tendency toward discrimination that disadvantages any segment of our people.

If there are worthy mandates that required funding that was not provided then it would be appropriate to do so. It should be remembered that Washington plays hard ball politics. Right now it is in a frenzy relative to 1996 elections, and every move is considered in that context. Congress is in a mood to cut, not pay. It would be naive to think that Congress will accept the role of leveling the taxes and then make ample block grants to the states without restrictions.

What Congress wants to do is shove problems onto the states under the guise of increasing local autonomy, then reduce federal grants to the states to aid reducing the federal deficit, and, very importantly, let the state and local governments deal with the outcry when the impact is felt.

🌲🌲🌲

## Education Test Scores Need Analysis
### 8-24-95

Raw statistics need analysis. To make an adverse judgment of the Minnesota K–12 public school system because certain Minnesota test scores rank below other states may fail to take into account important factors.

For example, presumably the scores of those who take the exam are averaged. What about dropouts who don't take the exams? If a state has only a 60% retention rate its students taking the exam may be a more selective group than that within a state with 80 or 90% retention. Minnesota has a high retention rate and this may be skewing some of the score comparisons.

Also, Minnesota has an extensive special education program for children with disabilities of various kinds. If these are included in testing it could affect comparisons with states doing less in this area. It certainly would affect results of children with mental disabilities. Minnesota not only has classes for the educable retarded but also for the trainable. All we mean to suggest is that there are many variables from state to state and not too much credence should be given to raw data without analysis.

A truer measure would be the result of the educational program—the quality of the graduates. In a recent comparison of college readiness test scores Wisconsin was first in the nation and Minnesota second. This is more typical of the traditional Minnesota standard. Our high school graduates are among the best prepared in the country for post secondary training.

There is certainly room for improvement in our public school system. By increasing its entry requirements the University of Minnesota had a strong and healthy impact on high school curricula and graduation requirements. Laws should be considered providing for percentages of faculty required with standards of training and experience so school districts don't overload with minimally trained teachers to save money.

When committees of experts have had opportunity to examine our educational institutions they have been complimentary and admiring. We shouldn't let raw and possibly faulty statistical comparisons shake our confidence in an outstanding corps of educators and administrators, monitored by dedicated school boards. Interested citizens can visit a school and make their own judgments.

# State's Economy Is Doing Well

11-30-95

Bureau of the Census figures for 1992 and 1993, released this week, reveal that Minnesota's economy is doing well. There are more people employed at higher average pay with a larger total payroll. There were 120,532 businesses in 1993, an increase of 2.6 percent over 1992. As of March 1993 there were 1,944,630 people employed in private jobs compared with 1,862,438 in March 1992, an increase of more than 82,000. These are impressive gains for one year and the trend has appeared to continue into 1994 and 1995. The total private payroll was $47.6 billion compared with $45.2 billion in l992, a gain of 5.7 percent in one year. Average pay went up 1.3 percent. Reports of down-sizing, layoffs and cutbacks that appear in the news make the solid gains all the more remarkable and reassuring. In east-central Minnesota, every county showed gains across the board in rates of pay, total employment and total payroll. A strong private sector makes possible a strong public sector of education, health and social services, court system, park provision, highways, sanitation, law enforcement and all the other elements of a strong society. A well-developed infrastructure is essential to progress in the private area. Minnesotans have demonstrated again and again their desire for strong public institutions and willingness to provide adequate support if they can be convinced of value for the investment and satisfactory performance by public officials. Confidence has been shaken in recent years and it is incumbent upon every public employee, elected or appointed, to be good examples of public service and active spokespersons for the service or function in which they are engaged. People who have worked closely with public agencies know that most public employees are exemplary and dedicated. The shirkers need to shape up or be weeded out. The structures and procedures can be reviewed and improved so people will recognize governnent as a helpful partner in the continuing effort for a healthy and happy society.

⚘ ⚘⚘ ⚘

## Minnesota Agriculture Seventh Nationally

12-14-95

Fewer farms, but bigger farms and increased productivity, keeps Minnesota a very important agricultural state—seventh in the nation after California, Texas, Iowa, Kansas, Nebraska, and Illinois. Intensive labor dairying is giving way to crop production, and poultry is gaining on hogs as the leading livestock industry and has passed fattened cattle. The Minnesota Planning Department just released a study based on the federal agricultural census for 1992. Minnesota produced $6.5 billion in agricultural products. It produced more sugar beets and green beans than any other state, was second only to North Carolina in marketing of turkeys, and second only to Wisconsin acres planted of sweet corn. We ranked third in oats and soybeans and in the number of farms producing $100,000 or more of farm produce. Milk price per hundredweight declined from $22 in 1978 to $13 in 1992. Competition from southern and southwestern states has been a factor as have better economic possibilities in crop areas. Some dairymen who have gone to cash-crop farming are among those working full time off the farm. Off-farm work is a big factor because of the definition of a farm—any operation producing $1,000 or more of agricultural product. Statisticians hate to change criteria because it destroys comparisons for a year at least, but to call a $1,000 producer a farm must certainly raise questions. Wouldn't a $10,000 figure make more sense? A $1,000 producer is more likely a hobby gardener, selling a little produce and earning a livelihood off the farm or from managing other assets. Minnesota has a remarkably well-balanced economy with its strong agriculture, income from other natural resources, industry, distribution, personal services and tourism. There are not many states that can rival Minnesota's diversity, which gives stability. We love our theatre of seasons but right now is not the best time to talk about it.

🌲🌳🌳🌲

## *A Mountain Of Money*
## *Brings Forth A Mouse*

### 3-7-96

Minnesota is about to join 17 other states that require passing of a competency test in order for students to receive a high school diploma. The standards being established by the new Department of Children, Families and Learning are pathetically low. Some $20,000,000 was spent on studies leading up to the present action. We cannot understand how so much could be spent on a study of this kind. Furthermore, the result is alarming in its lack of integrity and failure to realize what American students need and must achieve.

Starting next year the only requirements will be in reading and math, and if the student tests at an eighth grade level a diploma will be granted. What kind of a standard is that? A year or two later, tests for writing will be added, at the same level of accomplishment. Originally it was intended to include geography, science, health and government but all four have been dropped from the testing program. In justifying their omission Commissioner Bruce Johnson said such tests would only measure what they knew, not what they could use. It sounds like preparation for $4.25-an-hour jobs at a fast food place rather than education for a good job in a world of high technology, or even for responsible American citizenship. No mention is made of comparable standards in Japan, Germany, England, France, Sweden or other high technology countries. The fact is that American college freshmen and women find it hard to compete with students from other countries—they come better prepared. Concern for adequate development of children should begin before they are born by ensuring proper pre-natal care and lifestyle impact. It should recognize the critical period of early child development from birth to three, that more formal education should begin at three, not five, and a really fine education should not only include years of basics plus science, geography, music, fine arts, world history and language, but a four-year liberal arts education followed by professional training. That would be preparation for a contributing significant life in the 21st century world. Young people should not be given evidences of accomplishment they have not achieved. The department of Children, Families and Learning betrays the Minnesota tradition with its misleading standards of testing.

*An alumnus of the University of Minnesota, the author has served that institution in a variety of capacities, including Chairman of the Board of Regents. The welfare of the University and the system of education in Minnesota at all levels is a recurring theme in his weekly editorials.*

# Nurture University, Don't Manage It

### 6-13-96

Management suggests authority—laws in government, orders in corporations, edicts in religion. A true university has a different tradition. Someone has called a university a community of scholars, brought together to study and teach. It seeks consensus through committees. It doesn't make its members rich nor gain power over others. It was, and still is, the fragile fabric that encases the love and transfer of learning. It operates by consensus, not fiat. It is an imperfect human institution but has worked remarkably well.

Central to a great university is academic freedom, the right to pursue knowledge and express new perceptions however they may challenge the conventional wisdom. What would be insubordination in a corporation or heresy in a religion is freedom of inquiry and expression—the heart of a university. It requires intense devotion to the pursuit of new knowledge and courage to declare and defend it. It also takes public wisdom and understanding to permit it to exist.

To enable some scholars to devote their undivided attention to their studies, research and teaching, they are assured of their income which also relieves them of economic retribution for their ideas. In modern terms it is tenure, hard won and voted by one's peers. It is not a license for lassitude but freedom from insecurity to pursue one's work with concentration. There can be abuses which a faculty is willing to correct, but no board of regents should seek to impose drastic changes. The faculty is a better arbiter than any board of regents in guiding university policy. The board's job is to nurture, not to manage, and to generate public understanding and support. Scholars generate great wealth for their societies, they don't accumulate much for themselves. Tenure is an important part of the fabric that sponsors fine teaching, research and the civil pursuit of new truth.

Nils Hasselmo, president of the University of Minnesota, is an ideal example of the scholar administrator. He has presided, with great skill, at a time of restructuring, reallocation of resources and guiding these changes through complicated systems of consideration and approval. Much of it is done as Hasselmo's administration draws to an end. As a new president is sought, it is the time for all elements to rally behind the university, recognizing the great institution it is and the tremendous contributions it has made. It is not only the educational fountainhead of the state but the economic engine that has created companies, stimulated agriculture, developed the talents of hundreds of thousands of students and in some way touched and enhanced the lives of everyone in the state.

# Fifty States Or One Nation

12-6-84

In the struggle over the federal budget that is beginning in Washington there is much more at stake than the amount to be spent on various programs or the extent to which the federal deficit can be brought under control. There are also ideological differences over the role government should play and particularly the federal government in areas of social service and education.

Quite apart from the money involved there are those who feel the federal government has played too great a role in the lives of the people and many programs should be cut back or eliminated and leave it to the people working through state and local government to determine what should be done there and to what degree people should be left to their own or private volunteer resources.

This issue was faced to a degree in the first Reagan administration but with the election result hailed by some as a mandate plus the effect of people's concern over the deficit much more pressure for change can be expected now.

When our nation was founded there was an enormous fear of the power of central government and our first national organization was a federation of states with very little central authority or responsibility. It did not work very well, particularly when the states began to inhibit trade between the states. A convention was called to resolve the problem and that became our constitutional convention which drafted the basic document under which, with amendments adopted over the years, we still operate.

To meet the crisis of the great depression President Franklin Roosevelt with the almost unanimous support of the Congress launched the country on a new course of federal responsibility for the welfare of individuals caught in economic situations beyond their control and a complicated program of "categorical aids" which mandated programs to the states, some of which were totally or partially federally financed and some not.

Also federal aid to education, a fiercely contested issue before its adoption, has grown to be a major support of educational equality throughout the country.

Very complex practical and theoretical issues are involved. Basically the current argument for reversing the trend of fifty years is that the programs are completely out of hand cost wise, that they could be administered more efficiently locally and waste eliminated, and the people locally should decide what they want to do and how much they want to spend and have the control. Some programs, such as Social Security, are so well entrenched that public officials, at all levels, are pledged to make no change.

Those who tend to favor federal programs argue that this is one nation and educational opportunity and social welfare benefits should not vary from state to state but have certain basic standards available to all people wherever they happen to live. Opponents of "states' rights" say, "a state should not have the right to keep a problem at home and do nothing about it."

The Congress will probably not make wholesale changes but the issue is well defined and it will be up to individuals throughout the country who pay enough attention and care enough about what is going on to communicate with their representatives and senators in Washington.

Attached to this, of course, is the whole question of military spending, which President Reagan and the administration do not want to reduce.

Surfeited with politics from the long election campaign people may now turn away from the matter. If they do, they may be surprised at what happens. There are crucial issues at stake and the determination can be with the people if they but make their wishes known.

⁂

# Education And The Home

12-20-84

A child gets off the school bus, goes to the door of the home, fumbles for the key pinned to his or her coat, unlocks the door and enters an empty house. It's scary, the child says, and indeed it is, in more ways than one.

Two thirds of all women of child bearing age are now in the work force and the percentage continues to increase. The conviction is that one income is not sufficient to provide the needs of a family in today's world. In some families adjustments in life styles are made so one parent can stay home and concentrate on care of the family, but that is the exception.

There is no question that an additional burden is placed on the school when both parents of school children work. Instead of a close partnership with the school in matters of discipline, homework, after school activity, attitudes, the growing tendency is to expect the school to do the entire job and to look to day care centers to provide for the pre-school child.

Meanwhile, overwhelming evidence is accumulating on the importance of the early years in a child's development—educationally, temperamentally, socially. Some would claim that by the time a child is three much of its future is already structured. What happens to a society that neglects making the most of those important years?

One cannot help but wonder what the net contribution to a family budget the second income is if subtractions are made for all the tax deductions, the cost of transportation, the cost of clothes and grooming, the cost of child care and other expenses stem from their economic status. They stand out in believing most people would try to take advantage of you; they believe least that hard work is most important in getting ahead, though a majority are of that opinion. They are the most abstemious in our population. They want government to do more, and to reduce income differences.

Except for the Blacks and Hispanics there is much less ethnic division in our population, the differences relate more to economic status. These studies indicate that economic well being was the big deciding issue in the recent election and swept aside all other considerations and issues.

One graph showed the perfect correlation between the employment rate and President Reagan's approval rating. As employment bumped along at its low in late 1982 so did Reagan's approval. As employment improved in 1983, so did the president's approval until the latter part of 1984 as employment leveled off the presidents approval began to decline.

The ethnic and social grouping that Franklin Roosevelt put together so effectively in the 30s and 40s had little relevance in the

80s which would account for the Mondale failure despite all the leadership support from traditional grouping.

When people were asked about their father's education, 55% had less than high school, 26% were high school graduates, 8% had some college, 12% were college graduates. When asked about their own education the results were 30% less than high school, 34% high school graduate, 20% some college, 17% college graduate. Our educational job is evident when 64% of our people have only high school education or less.

Forty percent of our people think of themselves as moderate, 26% as liberal, and 33% as conservative. As we come to the end of another year there can be some pride to be part of a nation where 32% of the people think of themselves as very happy with life, and 55% pretty happy and only 14% judging themselves as "not too happy."

## *Let's Hear It For The Farmers*

2-21-85

Sitting with publishers, editors and their spouses at the Minnesota Newspaper Association convention we were surprised at how little support there was for doing something about the plight of Minnesota farmers. Mostly the comments centered around the farmers in difficulty bringing trouble on themselves by over expansion or other kinds of misjudgment and mismanagement and that government should not be looked to, constantly, for bailout.

One thing that should not be overlooked in that overly harsh judgment is that our farming industry, overall, has led the world in improved farming technology and production of food at the lowest cost achieved anywhere. No workers on earth work fewer hours to earn their food than does the American worker. Included in that farming industry are the small and the large, the efficient and the less efficient, the prosperous and the marginal.

If any substantial part of that industry were to be forced out of production and the supply of food be only slightly less than demand the consumers could experience a jolt in what would happen to food prices. It may be in the consumers best interest to support the marginal producers in order to be sure of an adequate supply and to avoid the massive price increases that could attend a shortage.

Farmers could probably live without governmental support if they could also be free of government interference. American farmers can compete with any producers in the international market if given a chance to do so on even terms but the U.S. government won't always let them do so. President Jimmy Carter prohibited the sale of grain to Russia, our international negotiators do not always do well by American agriculture, permitting subsidized agricultural products to enter our markets at cut prices, and agree to European common market practices that close out our producers.

In times of national emergency our farmers have geared up to produce all the food the nation and its defense forces wanted only to be forgotten when the emergency is over. Defense factories are treated better than American farmers. The factories are maintained on a standby basis, just in case.

In any field there are some performers who do well no matter what the conditions and some who find it hard to make it even when the situation is most favorable. In the case of food production we are concerned about a public policy that would let all but the most efficient fall by the wayside. We may get too efficient for our own good as consumers. It is not a question of protecting farmers but one of assuring an adequate food supply at the modest cost we have enjoyed for a long time and preserving a way of life that has contributed much to our society.

♣♣♣♣

# Assessing The Death Penalty
## 1-23-92

In a violent reaction to the growing number of awful crimes—mass murders, rapes, some of a particularly vicious nature—people understandably are calling for the death penalty for perpetrators of these terrible acts. It reflects the nature of the times—impatience with failure or deficiency and desire for instant solution. Many states have passed death penalty legislation and it is being urged upon Minnesota, which has not had it for more than 80 years.

For a number of reasons we feel Minnesota should not move in that direction. First of all, there is no evidence that death penalties deter the crimes they are meant to punish and discourage. Neither does that process of dealing with the worst criminals save money as compared with life, imprisonment and no chance for parole. It is estimated that the whole procedure of reviews and appeals in the case of death penalty administration can cost as much as $3 million per person. There is always the chance an innocent person will be put to death. It can hardly be pointed to as the crowning achievement of a successful and caring society.

Two alternatives occur to us, one long range and the other more immediate. If these were fully carried out successfully we believe there would be a substantial reduction in crime of all kinds. First, the long range solution would be to commit ourselves and the resources to provide adequately for pre-natal care for all pregnant women with intensive effort to get them to follow life styles that assure birth of a healthy child. This to be followed by the recognition of the vital importance of love, parental attention, care, and medical service in the first three years of a child's life, as well as thereafter. Then a pre-school preparation so every child would have an equal chance at learning in a normal school situation. Finally, a school experience that recognizes the potential of every child and concentrates on achievement oriented education and preparation for a self supporting, contributing, and achieving later life. All this would include greater and required parental responsibility. We fail in many of these areas and some of the results are more to be pitied then condemned.

The more immediate solution is removal of people who threaten society and placing them in self supporting public industries with constant surveillance and no freedom. Minnesota has successful examples of such. In addition, something like the CCC camps of the 1930s should be established for high school age youth who are not in school, or not employed, so they are not on the loose and bound to get into trouble. Efforts would be made to orient them to successful schooling or employment. These two approaches would be efforts of which a society could be proud, positive in approach and promising of results.

# Science And Creationism

6-18-92

Once again, as so often in the past, people are pressuring public school authorities to require the teaching of "creationism" along with "evolution" in science classes.

Creationism is the doctrine of creation and development as told in the Bible. Fundamentalists believe the Bible is the literal word of God and is not to be questioned or "interpreted." Courts have held, time and time again that creationism is a religious interpretation and has no place in a public school curriculum but may be taught freely in a church environment.

Science is not the teaching of dogma; it is the search for truth. What is thought to be factual at any time is taught but research is encouraged to constantly search for new evidence.

We need to encourage more teaching of science in our public school curriculums for there is much that is known about our universe . In most curricula little science teaching is required. It is the work of science to teach the means of learning and research so new information may be constantly sought and added to the body of knowledge.

Particularly in our country of diverse religious belief, and ethnic origin, it is inappropriate for one group to seek to force religious dogma on others. No one Bible is accepted by all. We stand for freedom of inquiry, freedom of expression and freedom of religious practice. Anything that threatens that strikes at the heart of our nation.

# Bringing People And Jobs Together

## 3-11-93

A constant struggle for many families is to find the balance between family security, good educational opportunities, quality of life for family living and a good job without the burden of many miles of driving. Smaller towns frequently provide the family life desired but not enough of the quality jobs.

In efforts to develop a stronger economic base communities advertise in trade journals hoping to reach business executives considering new plant locations. Such ads will feature a desirable industrial park, available financing by development committees, sometimes available buildings on desirable terms and often mention of pleasant and attractive living features of the community. There is rarely, if ever, the kind of detail relative to the available work force that could be a decisive factor. The quality and quantity, of the local work force is frequently the single most important factor in the ultimate business decision on where to locate.

The smart community of the future will make a careful survey of the skilled workers in a community, identify their education, experience and skills and determine what percent are employed locally and what percent are underemployed or commute. In our community, or any other, the chances are that the quantity and quality of skilled talent available would be an eye opener as well as the high percent employed outside the community.

If a firm that is computer oriented learned that a community had 220 skilled computer operators and 80% were employed outside the community it would look like a natural for the operation looking for a location and needing 80 skilled computer operators. This community needs to make a detailed inventory of its work force and make it easier for the people who want to live here by bringing their jobs closer to home. The many benefits are obvious.

Commuters are more anxious than ever to see people and jobs closer together. Its not only talk of substantial increases in gas taxes but the increasing time loss and hassle of driving daily on ever more congested and dangerous highways. Any community that featured detailed information on the skills of its people instead of so much emphasis on industrial parks and buildings would attract attention of business leaders and commuters alike and be out in front in the battle for a brighter economic future for both people and community.

# Providing Equal Rights For Women
### 3-18-93

On March 22, 1972 the United States Senate passed the 27th amendment to the United States Constitution and sent the proposal to the states for ratification. The amendment prohibited discrimination on the basis of sex. Under the law seven years is provided for ratification. Hawaii was the first state to ratify. Others followed, 22, including Minnesota, by the end of the first year. When the seven year ratification period was about to expire and the required 38 ratifications had not been achieved the Congress did what it had never done before, it extended the ratification date to June 30, 1982. Even that did not get the job done. Only 35 states had ratified and the amendment failed of adoption. There is no guarantee of equal rights for women in the Constitution.

It may be that every state has provided the equal rights guarantee to women in such clarity that a constitutional amendment would now be considered an anachronism. Nevertheless, the fact is that if some state went berserk and passed some law discriminating against women and upset people attacked an act under the law as unconstitutional our Supreme Court would have to hold "there is no guarantee in our Constitution of equality under the law regardless of gender." Should not that long overdue provision in our constitution be added?

The last amendment to the constitution is No. XXVI providing 18 as the legal age. That was passed during the Kennedy administration, and some believe too hastily. One of the strong arguments for it was "if our young people are old enough to go to war to fight and die for their country they are old enough to participate in its decisions as adults." Some states have since raised the age for certain acts, such as the purchase of liquor from 18 to 21.

We would not suggest repeal of XXVI but we do think that XXVII should be revived and resubmitted to the states. We can find no valid reason for not doing this. If there is a reason that has escaped us—we would like to know.

# How Government Can Aid Job Creation

5-13-93

There are many ways state and federal government can aid job creation. Spending public money on created short term employment is the most expensive and least productive way. The best way is to create the environment that encourages private initiative to make investments, start companies, and finance the growth of smaller firms.

The basic environment is sound fiscal policy by the involved state or federal government. This means balanced operating budgets and controlled debt. Federally we fail wretchedly on this criteria, but Gov. Arne Carlson is making solid progress. Minnesota's credit rating is improving and its interest cost on debt is going down, even more than general interest rates.

Tax policy can have important and direct influence, negatively or positively. A lower tax rate on capital gains encourages venture capital investment. If the chance for return is higher, greater risk can be taken. If capital gain is taxed heavily investors are less apt to make venture capital commitments. It is the establishment and growth of small firms that creates the most jobs. Talk of singling out the "rich" for tax increases is very bad policy. In the first place, it is deceitful because you cannot finance government without broad participation and secondly, when any segment feels it is being singled out inequitably it moves to protect itself. With the talk of singling out the "rich" brokers of tax exempt securities quickly increased their selling efforts. So capital seeks protection instead of being invested where it would create jobs. Furthermore, any talk that encourages class distinctions and punitive tax policy may be politically effective with some people but most harmful economically and socially. It should be abhorred. Progressive taxation is fair, charging those with more income at higher rates, but presenting it as singling out one group to carry the whole burden is counter productive from every standpoint.

Keeping government programs, such as worker compensation, within reasonable limits and operated to avoid abuse is essential. At present there are so many auxiliary expenses in hiring a person that firms resort to part time employment to avoid the excessive burden of government cost on full time employees. Lawmakers don't look far enough ahead as to the results of laws passed, and what counter action will happen as a result. Simplifying regulation and regimentation would go far to encourage more employment.

It is not easy to run a business successfully and profitably. Those who think it is usually have not tried it. There needs to be a better partnership and communication between government and business—and business needs to put priority on worker well being and honest customer service to help create the better environment.

# An Approach To The Biggest Health Care Cost Problem

### 10-28-93

What really frightens national health care planners when they face the realities of the costs of providing universal health care is the cost of "long term care" which can also be called nursing home care. It is one thing to provide for illness, accident and occasional hospitalization, expensive as they can be, but when you undertake to pay for nursing home care, permanently, for year after year, with increasing services and costs it is a staggering burden with an average individual cost of $25 to $50 thousand a year. That one item could mount to a trillion dollars a year.

Only Minnesota and Hawaii have faced up to long term care and hence become the subject of a *New York Times* article singling them out for "moving a long way down the path to total health care." About 50 years ago Minnesota established a legislative policy that the needy elderly should have adequate health care at public expense. At first it was coupled with a "lien law" that provided for keeping track of the cost and recovering it from the covered person's estate, if there was one. That became unpopular and was repealed. A nursing home industry developed and families became less willing to keep the elderly at home. A doctor's recommendation was necessary to qualify for entry to the nursing home at public expense and if one doctor was unwilling another could be found.

Smaller families, smaller living quarters, rising costs of care all contributed to the rapid increase in nursing home care and the divesting of assets to meet the "indigent" test so the state would pay. Today Minnesota leads the country in number of nursing home beds per 100,000 population, 85% of all beds occupied are at public expense, and this item of cost is 80% of the whole human services budget. It is an enormous burden and squeezes everything else in the state budget.

A few years ago some public spirited people in St. Anthony Park of St. Paul started a "block nurse" program, a neighborhood effort to give some nursing and other attention to elderly people seeking to live independently. It was quickly evident that many older people (it is estimated 20% now in nursing homes) would much prefer to live independently if they had some help. Human Services Commissioner Natalie Haas Steffen has been quick to see the advantage and potential of the program. It has grown to be a funded professional service. For an expenditure of $3000 to $5000 annually the nursing home expense can be avoided or at least postponed and older people permitted to live happier lives. It does put more responsibility on family and relatives to take some interest and nursing home operators are not going to push it. But it is a way of saving large amounts of health care money if there is the public will to do it. Surely, in any national health plan, eligibility for public expense long term care must be very carefully structured and alternatives considered.

# A Continuing Struggle For Human Rights
### 1-20-94

It was in December of 1955 that Rosa Parks was arrested for violation of a local ordinance on segregated seating in public buses. Her act was a triumph of human dignity and self respect over bigotry. Martin Luther King Jr., pastor of a church in Montgomery Alabama, where the incident occurred, his associate Ralph Abernathy and the president of the Alabama chapter of the National Association for the Advancement of Colored People called a public meeting to protest. They urged people to boycott the bus company by avoiding use of the buses. That went on for a year before the bus company capitulated and segregated seating ended. King had become a national figure and the long civil rights struggle had started.

In January of 1957, approximately 60 black ministers met and formed the Southern Christian Leadership Conference and King became its president. Born in 1929, King was but 28 years old when he assumed this leadership and was soon meeting with Vice-president Nixon and President Eisenhower. He introduced the non-violent strategy into the civil rights movement and received a Nobel Prize.

In 1963 King led a march of 125,000 in Detroit, and on August 27, 250,000 gathered in Washington and King delivered the famous "I Have A Dream speech." On April 4, 1968, in Memphis, Tenn., he was struck with an assassin's bullet and died in a Memphis Hospital. He was 39 years old. As he had been its leader, King became the symbol of the entire civil rights effort and suggestions were made to memorialize him with a national holiday. It was established and is now observed annually on the Monday nearest his Jan. 15th birthday.

Wise leaders now tell their black brothers and sisters that future progress is more dependent on them, their use of freedom, their dedication to their community and their effort to move into the mainstream of economic well-being, than it is on changes in law. The opportunity is there. The King holiday is a time to recognize that we are all in this together and that until and unless all mankind has the benefits of freedom and justice it is not secure for anyone, anywhere. We can be thankful to Rosa Parks, to Martin Luther King Jr., and all others who lead the struggle to this day.

# Playing With Lethal Weapons

## 3-17-94

One of the most awesome weapons in the arsenal of the United States, or any other nation, is the ultimatum. It brings a nation to the brink of war. It says, do this or there will be an attack. The United States with the North Atlantic Treaty Organization and the United Nations said that to Serbia. Get your guns away from Sarajevo or turn them over to the United Nations or our planes will bomb. Serbia made partial compliance but the weapons remaining were not turned over to the United Nations. When the United Nations general in command was asked where he would be when the deadline passed said he would probably be in bed sleeping. It was evident there was no real intention to pursue the ultimatum. It was a powerful bluff. That is devastating to the integrity of the United States. Meanwhile suffering and death goes on in Bosnia and the U. S. now talks about a "peace keeping force." There is no peace to keep. Our nation should decide on a policy and then pursue it vigorously and decisively. The lack of that in Vietnam dragged it out to no conclusion and a disastrous effect on U.S. morale.

Now President Clinton has drawn out another lethal weapon. It is a policy process relating to international trade called Super 301. If our country feels it is being dealt with unfairly to the extreme by another nation's trade policy, it announces the implementation of Super 301. The offending nation is named and 18 months allowed for resolving the difficulty, following which, if unresolved, sanctions are imposed prohibiting importation of the other nation's products. To blockade a nation to keep material from going into it is an act of war. To impose sanctions forbidding importation of a nations goods is an act of trade war with the most serious implications.

Everyone knows Japan is the target. It is too serious a move to simply build the impression of a macho president. If Japan wanted to shoot a shell across our bow, it would begin dumping our bonds on the international market. Japan has purchased up to 30% of the bonds we sell to finance deficit and debt. We simply must get our financial affairs in better shape, or realize we must get along with our creditor nations. It's not smart to slap your banker in the face.

The Clinton administration cannot seem to get away from a political campaign syndrome of doing things to build image rather than facing up to the substantive responsibilities of the presidency. The integrity, safety and security of the nation is at sake—it is no time for international posturing.

## *Planning Comprehensive Care For Children*

### 9-29-94

The General Assembly of the United Nations has designated the first Monday in October as Universal Children's Day. It was first declared in 1933. By annual proclamation since 1928 the same day is identified as Children's Health Day in the United States. There are many stable homes where children are received, through birth or adoption, with loving and responsible care and which provide the environment to which every child is entitled. There are also a large number of social service agencies in our state which, through private and public financial support, provide excellent staff and material support to endeavor to ensure every child of essential care. However high the percentage of all children so reached we know there are large numbers of children in situations that fall far short.

Because the astronomical costs that can attend publicly paid medical care for high risk children, the threat to our future as a society, as well as a proper public regard for the welfare of all children, child care should rank high in our concerns.

There has been enormous progress in research on early child development in the last 30 years. We know much more than we did about the importance of pre-natal care and the first three years of a child's life. During the same period so-called "permissive life styles" have resulted in an increasing percentage of children born out of wedlock, and most alarmingly, to single teenagers. Also use of tobacco, alcohol, other drugs during pregnancy is accelerating the number of tragically disadvantaged high risk babies.

Proper care begins before pregnancy with education and counseling on the responsibilities and serious consequences of child birth without maturity, readiness, resources and preparation by both father and mother. There should be more emphasis on sexual morality and less on "safe sex." Young people should visit hospitals treating high risk children to see what happens when life styles run rampant over good sense. There should be extensive education on needs of infants and very young children and the importance of continued parental love and care. Most of the social problems of later life have roots in unplanned and unwanted pregnancies, pre-natal neglect and inadequate home environment.

It is not enough to talk about "family values." We should do something specific. What is needed is a comprehensive survey of each county, leading to state review of what is needed to realistically cope with the problem and then the willingness to give it the resources, both personal and public, that it deserves.

♠♣♠♣♠

# Crime And Crime Prevention
## 10-27-94

It is not surprising that concern for personal safety is a major contemporary issue. Incidence of crime has grown so widespread, even among young juveniles; brutal, vicious, personal attacks are every day occurrences; deaths are caused by drunken drivers; drug related incidents are frequent—simple personal safety is a primary daily concern of many people. The demand is for tougher penalties and longer mandatory sentences to stem the tide of growing crime, particularly by repeaters. We must immediately use every effort to provide safety for people. In addition, however, we must also look for longer range solutions, because, unfortunately, evidence does not support the hope that what we are doing will have long range beneficial results.

Our efforts and massive expenditures will be futile if, in addition to directing strong attention to the immediate problem, we do not also address the long range sources of crime. That goes to the whole range of poverty, deprivation, discrimination, ignorance, illiteracy, dependency, chronic unemployment, family breakdown, violence, child abuse, and all other conditions that warp personalities, develop societal hatreds, and trigger all manner of harmful behavior. We could certainly use more research on why conditions occur and what are the most successful means of breaking the destructive cycle.

We now jail more people per 100,000 of population than any other nation in the free world. It is a costly operation and is growing at an increasing rate. Can churches assume more of a community responsibility using their facilities more completely for parenting classes, guidance and fun, particularly for unreached young people? How can we make it possible for mothers to spend the first few years of a child's life loving and mothering it at home? Should such organizations as the national Boys and Girls Clubs organizations reach out to smaller communities? What can our community do to rescue young people from an environment that most assures future lives of anti-social conduct? While struggling to cope with immediate problems of crime and public safety, we must somehow realize that ultimately we must come up with a longer range solution—happy, fulfilling lives of self-esteem and law abiding success for all.

## Just What Is Going On?

12-29-94

Year end is a time for carefree celebration, enjoyment of family and friends, some review of the year past, with plans and resolutions for the future. Any review of 1994 must challenge anyone because of the many cross currents and the clear evidence of dissatisfaction with the state of affairs and a desire for change.

It is strange to hear talk of the economy getting "over heated," the need to raise interest rates to ward off inflation, at the same time that a large county seeks bankruptcy protection to work out financial problems, food shelves cannot keep up with demand, of "sizing down" of many firms, of stores closing, and of taxpayer revolt on school levy referendum votes; The sweeping changes brought about by the last election do not reflect prosperity. While expenditures for public services are under attack, gambling casino revenues are figured in the billions, and entertainment and athletic events at high ticket prices play to packed stands. Everything is so mixed up one cannot help but wonder what is going on.

One major development of recent years is irrefutable. The gap between the rich and poor is widening, and the less fortunate group is growing larger and reaching up into the middle class blue collar workers. It is estimated that jobs in manufacturing, construction and related fields constituted about 40% of the work force at the end of World War II and is now down to 25%. Furthermore, rates of pay have actually decreased in many union contracts. Overall, from a purchasing power standpoint, real wages have been going down for years. Election time talk about government expenditures and taxes is a focal point but the real problem goes much deeper and particularly affects men and their ability to make enough to support a family. Men are angry and frustrated with their inability to cope with the present situation. Women head of households have similar economic problems but it was a major movement of blue collar men that affected the degree of change in the election.

Part of what is going on is caused by global economic forces. We lost a huge part of our automobile industry to global competition and aided the outflow by our own purchase of foreign cars. To compete worldwide, many adjustments are being made. Lifting the world standard of living will help protect our own. With all the problems and confusion we are a favored nation; we are fortunate. However, it is going to take farsighted leadership, and reordering of priorities—in business, finance and industry as well as government—and a sensible, responsible citizenry to see us through the shoals ahead. If we make life better for those who have less, we will make America better for everyone.

## *Making The American Dream Come True*

### 1-5-95

New Year's Eve is a delightful time. It is pure joy. Thousands gather in Times Square, New York to cheer as the lighted ball descends to mark the moment the old year gives way to the new. Celebrations are everywhere and Channel 2 puts on a nostalgic Guy Lombardo revival for the older folk. Many welcomed the New Year in church. The bad could have been worse, we survived, next year will be better, we all love each other and high hopes reign. Tuesday Jan. 3 it's back to work.

Since 1932 people have tended to look to government for most solutions, particularly the federal government, where, the impression prevailed, that, somehow, money and benefits dispensed there didn't cost anyone anything. In more recent years higher taxes, debt, and deficits while purchasing power of paychecks declined caused increasing unease and distrust of government. Change was the cry in 1992 that swept Clinton in, to the presidency. Dissatisfaction with him brought another cry for change and has given the Republicans control of Congress.

The well being of most workers is more directly influenced by policies and philosophy of the local employer. In Minnesota and in other parts of the country there is a shifting in priorities away from making money as the sole purpose of business endeavor. For long range survival and success it is necessary, it is held, to place more emphasis on customer retention and service and employee satisfactions. If the only consideration is short range "bottom line" or net profit, the temptation is to minimize concern for the customer and the employee and to make "tough decisions" that can increase profit short range, harm employee interests and threaten the company, long range. Forward looking business leaders are sensing that they can have considerable influence on the temper of the country, as well as on the future of their own companies by realigning priorities. Financial analysts of public companies concentrate entirely on comparative short term earnings records. Builders of strong companies are resisting that pressure in favor of long range values with increasing customer concerns, employee development, and concern for social and community consequences of their decisions. Thoughtful investors are beginning to see the point. Our country is shaped more by what we do as individuals than what Congress does. Congress does not initiate, it reflects the public.

Enlightened self interest by the business leadership of the country may do more to bring stability to our nation than any shaking up Congress can devise. It is encouraging, in Minnesota particularly, that a more socially conscious business leadership is already making a difference in many lives.

# Balance Budget First,
# Then Consider Amendment

1-25-95

Congressional leaders who call for a constitutional amendment that would require the federal budget to be balanced, while unwilling to indicate how they would accomplish a balanced budget, reveal the fundamental weakness in their proposal. Passing a proposal for our constitutional amendment would give the impression of making a major step toward a balanced budget and politics is a game of perceptions.

Of prime concern to representatives and senators in Washington is the 1996 election—can the Republicans keep control of Congress, can Clinton retain the presidency, who will be the Republican candidate, can first term representatives and senators get re-elected? What will be the mood and perceptions of the people then? There was a conclusion that a tax cut was uppermost in the minds of the people and Clinton and the Congress were in a virtual bidding contest for the people's support on the tax cut issue. A recent much publicized poll has caused some reconsideration.

When asked which they preferred, a tax cut or a balanced budget, 58% said a balanced budget, 35% said a tax cut. Rep. James Oberstar asked a similar question in a newsletter to his constituents and 80% of the respondents favored a balanced budget. It is significant that people are awakening to the seriousness of the situation and are now of a mind to sacrifice immediate personal advantage for the broader general good. That gets back to the amendment issue. Whatever value a constitutional amendment would have would be in preventing an unbalanced budget once balance has been reached. There are more current issues to decide.

A big credit to Mexico is a subsidy to American business—is this the time? Can we defer a big military build-up? Gradually it is becoming apparent that we don't have to cut essential programs, we just have to slow down the increases. Serious Congressional decisions now, with careful consideration could turn the situation around. America wants facts and figures—and complete openness, no "off the budget" items. A good beginning would be the status of foreign loans and grants, their record on repayment, the budget for this year and proposed for next year. People are sick of perceptions and want action and measurable results. The constitutional amendment can wait.

🌲🌲🌲🌲

# Affirmative Action Is Not Discrimination
## 2-23-95

California has an initiative on the ballot that would ban affirmative action programs and a conservative talk show host is supporting the idea, with the comment that hiring should be on merit only. That misses the fact that laws became necessary because hiring was not being done equally on merit regardless of race, color, creed or gender. Affirmative action seeks to achieve equal opportunity.

In 1957 Minnesota became the fifth state in the country to pass a Fair Employment Practices Act to assure equality among all people in seeking employment, It required that hiring be done without regard to race, color, creed or gender. Organizations were encouraged to establish affirmative action programs to affirm the idea conveyed in the legislation. The purpose was equality not reverse discrimination.

Fair employment legislation and affirmative action programs have helped but not been completely successful. The rate of unemployment among blacks is higher than among whites and that does not take into consideration the underemployment of many skilled black men and women. White women have made strides too but are still not as readily employed as men, and the public mood is certainly reflected in the tendency to elect less qualified men over better qualified women. Other groups would not testify that discrimination has been eliminated in employment or anywhere else.

Those who support the idea that affirmative action discriminates against whites are revealing their bias that any white person is better than any black or other minority and thus not hiring the white is discrimination. By hard work, successful studies, and improved attitudes and self esteem, minorities are equipping themselves to compete and are doing well. It is not so long ago that blacks were barred from professional sports and look at what has happened on merit when the barriers were removed.

Surely hiring should be on merit, but jobs should be equally available to all regardless of race, color, creed or gender. Affirmative action to provide that equality of opportunity is still needed.

# Beating Swords Into Plowshares

## 3-23-95

U.S. agricultural policy has gone through two phases in recent history, neither one remarkably successful. In the earlier version national policy established price floors to protect producers. If markets threatened to go below support levels, the federal government stepped in and bought commodities. This program led to huge federal stocks of corn, wheat, butter, cheese, dried milk, casein and other supported products. Government storage bins sprouted all over the country. Ultimately with insufficient outlet for the surpluses the program had to end.

National policy then was directed at reducing production. Cows were purchased and slaughtered to reduce milk production. Government began to pay farmers not to produce through "set aside" acres, conservation plots and other designations which took land out of production. That program is now under review in Congress with the axe ready to chop.

If we decided to do so, we could combine a full production agricultural program with a peace effort with economic advantage to our own country and the world? There are, obviously, large unmet food needs at home and abroad. With access to world markets, a diplomatic task, our agricultural industry needs no governmental support. It can compete with agricultural producers anywhere.

We are the world's largest producers of military weapons. It is a nefarious business and we ought to get out of it. Agricultural full production at world dollar exchange rates would generate prosperity in rural America and enormous demand for farm equipment which arms plants could produce. Filling that need would provide employment for workers now employed in arms production.

There would be difficulties and complications. In the process of policy making the first priority is to decide on the goal. Second comes the program to achieve it, not lost energy discussing why it cannot be done. Releasing full agricultural potential and converting weapons plants to peaceful pursuits would help bring prosperity to all areas. Vision and courage are needed in high places.

# A Tax Cut Now Makes No Sense

### 3-30-95

Some members of Congress would like to go home and run for reelection on a "we cut your taxes" platform. It would be a disservice to the public interest and should be discouraged. Gov. Arne Carlson has spoken out against it. More than ever before people are aware of the operating deficit and the constantly mounting public debt and want something done about it. Those pushing for a tax reduction cannot come up with enough savings to cover it, and much of what they recommend to pay for it comes at the expense of the poor.

When a tax cut bill gets out on the floor, politically motivated amendments are offered to broaden its application. What is even worse is that it becomes a "Christmas tree" on which to hang tax cut ornaments for special interests or even individual corporations. A proposal for a dependency increase for those with a household income of $60,000 would be amended to $200,000. Under present national financial problems it would be completely irresponsible.

Polls indicate that people are more interested in true budget balancing than tax reduction. The idea that a tax reduction will stimulate the economy so more jobs will be created and more revenue brought in than before has been exploded. It was "voodoo economics" 25 years ago and still is. Interest on our national debt accounts for 18% of the national budget. The debt continues to grow and interest rates are going up. The degree of international concern is reflected in the decline of the dollar to a record low on foreign exchange markets despite strong efforts to support it.

Some have said we could balance the budget by simply slowing down the rate of increase in expenditure. That fails to give adequate weight to the increase in population. If school population increases by 4% and appropriations by 3%, the per pupil provision is cut. An increase in dollar amounts over a previous period is not always a real increase.

However approached there is no justification for a tax cut now. There is an enormous task ahead to get our national financial affairs in order. That undertaking should be taken seriously and responsibly.

# Do We Need A Flag Burning Amendment?

## 7-13-95

A few incidents of burning the American flag as a political protest and a Supreme Court decision that held such acts to be within our protected freedom of speech have so outraged Americans that some Congressmen feel led to propose a constitutional amendment prohibiting any desecration of our national emblem and providing penalties for doing so.

There is no question that the burning of an American flag is deeply offensive. It is so offensive that, with all its attention getting, it injures rather than enhances any cause with which it is connected. It has happened only rarely and is a problem hardly worthy of a constitutional change. One wonders if proponents are not themselves seeking political advantage by capitalizing on an issue that captures some peoples' attention and emotion.

Do we want to send a message to the world that it takes a special constitutional provision to protect our flag? There are better ways to solve that relatively minor problem. Two problems of enormous dimension that are growing worse need massive attention. They are crime and poverty. It should be clear that incarcerating the largest percentage of its people of any nation in the free world, building more and more prisons for punishment and release is a failed approach and yet we continue to pour more and more billions into it. We need new approaches of indefinite custody for repeat criminals in a self supporting rehabilitative environment. We also need to get the mentally ill into treatment centers instead of wandering homeless, a threat to themselves and others.

# Immigrants Should Become Americans

### 3-19-96

When thousands upon thousands of immigrants came to the United States in the late years of the 19th and early years of the 20th centuries, many of them our parents and grandparents, they sought a new life in a new land. They did not seek to transplant their homeland. That they left behind. They no longer thought of themselves as Norwegian, French, Italian or whatever—they wanted to become Americans and share in the freedom and opportunity that characterized their new home. They kept their culture. The Irish kept St. Patrick's Day but shared it with others so it became everyone's joy. There was assimilation and integration. No one talked of English as a second language. It was the language of public schools, shops, stores. Native tongues lingered on in church services and family affairs but was very much gone in one generation. An American is a definable, recognizable and distinctive human being. In any country from among a nationally diverse group of tourists the locals can easily pick out the Americans. They have a confident, friendly outgoing way about them that makes them identifiable just as other nationalities have attractive features that distinguish them. American society is not an amalgamation of many identifiable preserved national groups but a fusion of what all have brought into a distinctive nationality we call American. It is important we keep it that way. In recent years immigrants have had different ideas. They want schools conducted in the language they brought with them and speak of English as a second language. They form political organizations to further their own nationalistic ideas. If they want to transplant their native land, would it not be better for them to stay in that native land? Many are illegal immigrants whose only goal was economic and are not concerned with social integration. This is not a major problem in Minnesota but a big national problem that should concern all Minnesotans. The world is filled with examples of religious or political balkanization. America is one nation, indivisible. We can welcome people from all nations, welcome the rich diversity that their contributions provide. We can encourage the retention of native cultures and traditions but expect, with all the help needed, as the first priority, the acceptance of a new nationality, a new language, a new set of values, a new loyalty, the blessing and responsibility of a new freedom—and the strong desire to become Americans in the finest sense of the word.

♣ ♣♣ ♣

## *A Time For Confident, Bold, Progressive Action*

### 4-3-96

It has been well said that those who fail to study history are destined to repeat it. When Rome was at the height of its power, having destroyed all its external enemies, it turned to internal bickering, division and self-destruction. This led to its decline and fall. In 1907, a panic brought our country to near collapse when years of finance and industry's power-driven greed and wanton neglect of human concerns brought crippling strikes and loss of public confidence. In the early 1930s a failure of states and nation to cope with economic stagnation and human misery led to a depression that brought incredible havoc to our country and its people.

The United States of America is at the zenith of its wealth, power and influence. It is the envy of the rest of the world. People risk their lives to escape from their own countries and enter ours. Yet we are gripped with a public discontent. We are the lowest-taxed country in the Western world, yet we feel so overtaxed that every candidate for state or federal office feels compelled to promise to raise no taxes and to cut "wasteful spending." We tend to demoralize teachers and other dedicated public servants.

Two hundred years ago we decided a confederation of sovereign states would not work and went to a stronger federal government. A complicated alternative, imperfect, but better, has emerged. But now there are those who seek to dismantle federal policy and turn decision-making back to the states. Is there someone who would like to debate that a nation of 50 sets of state laws is a better way to face the global 21st century than a unified nation of common laws and standards?

It is time we came to our senses, appreciate all we enjoy that has been put together painstakingly by generations of careful work. We can enter a new century not picking ourselves to pieces but recognizing our strengths, our blessings as a people and reach out in the years ahead with a helping hand of world leadership to aspiring peoples and nations. The goal would be to help us all build peace, mutual concern and respect; and move into a sunlight of progress instead of wrapping the United States in a shroud of selfish discontent, isolation and blindness to the incredible opportunity for moving with boldness and confidence.

There are improvements and changes to be made but they should be done in the spirit of building on a successful past, with particular regard for those who have not done well in the past. We want them in the mainstream of a strong, united nation where every citizen has a place in the sunshine of prosperity.

# THE WORLD

## *An Historic Advance In Electricity*

6-4-87

While most of the country was preoccupied with accounts of the extra curricular activities of Gary Hart and Jimmy Bakker physicists of the world have been at a high pitch of excitement over a terrific development in the field of electricity.

Since the discovery and development of electrical energy, its generation, distribution and use has been one of the greatest boons to mankind. The interruption of electrical service, even for a short time, causes enormous inconvenience. With all its contributions, it has had some limitations.

When electrical current is passed through metal wire it loses some of its efficiency. For years the idea of super conductivity— passage without loss—has intrigued scientists. It was known to be possible but in metals cooled to extremely low temperatures, too low for practical applications. Suddenly researchers in different private and public institutions have discovered that ceramic type materials made up of copper oxide and elements such as yttrium and barium have raised the temperature at which there could be super conductivity. While still cold by any lay criteria, superconductivity is accomplished quite readily with liquid nitrogen. Some scientists are now speaking of reaching it at room temperature.

Not all of the implications are clear and some obstacles to full utilization of the new technology remain but there is unanimity in appraising the importance of the new discoveries. It will enable waste free transmission of electricity, the use of much larger magnetic coils for generating and storing electricity. New generations of computers are made possible.

If we could now come up with an inexpensive way to generate nuclear energy by fusion (the clean way) instead of by fission (the dirty and dangerous way) we would probably solve our energy problems for a very long time to come.

⁂

# This Century's Greatest Contribution
## 8-10-89

As we approach the end of the 20th century there will be increasing summaries and appraisals of the greatest accomplishments of this 100 year period. One fact that must command special attention is that this century has added 30 years to life expectancy at birth in the United States. That represents a greater gain than in all the rest of human history. Life expectancy in 1985—the latest year for which figures are available—is 71 years for men and 78 for women. Thirty years of additional life, on the average, is an incredible accomplishment of a society.

Seeking reasons we would immediately turn to the advances in medical technology—antibiotic drugs, surgery, transplants, prosthetic devices, implants—what a long list could be made to say nothing of elimination of the threat of certain diseases. Research in medicine has been an enormous contributor.

But not the only one, Sanitation—purification of water systems, development and extension of sewer systems, has played an important role. Safety in industry, agriculture and every day life has made a difference. Individual concern for nutrition has been a factor, and the role of food producers in developing wholesome food in abundance. Someone could do an interesting book "Adding Years to Life" to give us pride in this enormously positive result of this century.

One of the results is the increasing number of centenarians, people of 100 years of age or more. In 1980 there were 14,200 in the entire country. In just five years that number nearly doubled to 25,400. By the year 2000 it is expected to quadruple to 108,000.

Since 1950 the population 65 and over has more than doubled, the number of people 85 and over has increased almost five times, and the number of centenarians has grown by 10 times. Some may judge our 20th century harshly but we should not forget that it has contributed many years to our lives, and years of better health, better circumstances and opportunity for an even better future.

# Living With Islam

8-6-92

As the world grows smaller through communication technology and modern means of travel, and economies become globally oriented, it becomes increasingly important that we learn to accept one another, live and work together despite differences that can be substantial and fundamental. As enlightened as Minnesota is we have problems with ethnic, racial and religious differences and have to continue to work to maintain a society where people of diverse backgrounds can live together with mutual respect and in safety and peace.

One of the challenges of our future in the world is learning to live with peoples whose religion is Islam, and maybe an even greater challenge, helping them to learn to live with us. There is a struggle going on in the Islamic world between the fundamentalists and those inclined to accept features of western culture. Algeria is a case in point. It had been moving toward what we would call modernization in status of women, education, life styles, and attitude toward the rest of the world. Fundamentalists do not approve of all this and have been growing in numbers. In a recent free election the fundamentalists were in the majority but the army stepped in and kept them from taking control. Despite the strictest military curfew and control the head of state was recently assassinated. A religious civil war could break out at any time.

The fundamentalists of the Islam religion are growing in numbers and through democratically run free elections are taking over governments. If we find it impossible to find an acceptable working basis with them we could face many years of "cold war" relationships. Holy wars to stamp out the infidels or force their conversion was the Islamic way for centuries. In recent years, as in Iran, they would give lip service to democracy but act differently when in power. Saddam Hussein is not a religious leader as yet—a reason the amazing assembly of Arab nations against him was possible. Our relationship with him is outside this longer range consideration of how we treat with Muslims throughout the world. Here at home Islam is the fastest growing religion in the United States, by conversion as well as immigration and will soon be the third largest religious group in the country.

Is there a way to find accommodation with the Muslim fundamentalists who are now in the ascendancy? We have a Naval Academy, a West Point (army academy) and an Air Force Academy. Isn't it about time we established a Diplomacy Academy to develop highly skilled professional representatives to seek peaceful solutions to some of these problems with the same dedication and investment with which we plan for war?

# World Forces At Work
### 10-8-92

While the United States struggles with one of the most confused and confusing national elections in its history, while new east European nations work for identity and survival, while European nations are frightened at erosions of national power the elements most affecting life in the 21st century are not nationalistic but international and global in their direction.

While U. S. politicians debate as if we can solve our economic problems by government action, the fact is that the economic welfare of the American people, in today's world, depends on how well trained, serious, and productive our work force is, and how creative our management teams are to compete with people in the rest of the world. Those are factors primarily of private determination. If we had the share of the automobile, optics, and electronic market, to name a few, that we once had, U.S. economic activity would be much higher than it is.

It was most significant that French voters approved the Maastricht Treaty that moves toward European unity even though there will be short range disadvantages and dislocations to some portions of the population. It was similarly important that a Canada, Mexico, U.S. free trade pact has had preliminary approval though it has some obvious short range disadvantages. It was also remarkable that President Bush called for an expansion of the United Nations role in international peace keeping functions.

World radio, television and electronic communication provide people everywhere with better understanding of one another and an awareness of what takes place anywhere in the world. Travel and movement of merchandise by air makes the produce and products of the world readily available everywhere. If we could but turn our minds away from petty internal differences and struggles for advantage and think what could happen if all the peoples of the world participated in an improvement in food supply, health care, education, housing and all the other factors that make up a decent standard of living we would have an economic surge beyond anything ever conceived. Pockets of poverty, restrictions of opportunity, social problems that develop from unemployment, deprivation, and neglect in our own country would vanish as our people were caught up in a program of peace and prosperity for all.

People and nations which early catch the vision will benefit the most, those who selfishly grasp more tightly what they have will lose out in the end. A new world is coming! Its impact on individual nations may relate more to the people's understanding, acceptance and influence than on leadership initiative. People of the United States have every reason to be out there in front—if they so will it. There is no assurance as yet that they will.

# Where The Jobs Are Going

## 12-3-92

For its December 14 cover story *Fortune Magazine* features "The New Global Work Force" and calls attention to "Look Who's Getting the Jobs." It reviews the establishing of manufacturing plants in many parts of the world by U. S. firms. The two main criteria for location is a growing market to be served and the availability of highly skilled personnel. Lower wage rates can also be a factor but not nearly to the extent that many Americans believe. In some countries the average pay for jobs in manufacturing plants is higher than it is here.

An example of a U.S firm's international plant given was that of Hewlett Packard in Mexico with a design team made up entirely of advanced degree people, developing products for sale throughout the world. Minnesota's 3M is also featured as a firm sensitive to the global forces changing ways of doing business and recognizing new areas of rapidly developing opportunity.

As one observer stated, the rest of the world is catching up. One field is in education where in several countries children go to school more hours per day and more days per year than U. S. children do and come to U.S. colleges better trained and better able to compete in our country and in our language with the young people from our school systems. They go home as eager and highly skilled professionals.

United States firms, in 1991, doubled or more than doubled investments in manufacturing facilities as compared with 1985 in Britain, China, Germany, India, Jamaica, Japan, Mexico, Singapore and substantially increased them in many other places. Other countries' industries are doing the same so in all those places job growth is greater than in the U.S. Meanwhile foreign countries are buying up U.S. companies, one reason being the immensity of the U. S. market and the other because U.S. prices are cheap in terms of some foreign currencies. It is a rapidly changing world and U.S. national policy must be globally oriented.

Even future personal plans must take into account global changes and global opportunities. Students might well consider where the opportunities will be in the future and learn the language of that country to be prepared for employment opportunities through graduate training. Nothing could be more short sighted for our country than to cut back on educational opportunities for our young people and deny accessibility through high tuition.

# Third World Wages In First World Countries

7-22-93

One of the concerns about the North American Free Trade Agreement is that cheap labor in Mexico will take good jobs away from skilled workers in the United States. The first key fact is that labor cost is not determined so much by wage rates as by productivity. Generally speaking, highly skilled and highly paid workers are so much more productive than the uneducated and unskilled that labor cost of production is lower with the best workers.

Uneducated, unskilled, illiterate Mexican workers are not going to compete with skilled American workers. However, if those unskilled and uneducated are eager to learn and apply themselves, they can acquire knowledge and skills and even surpass U. S. workers if they win the competition of learning and growth.

A recent poll of Americans indicated that 44% did not know what NAFTA was. If we neglect the health and education of our young people and don't foster their interest in and acquaintance with world affairs, and their need to compete with workers everywhere, we can expect to become a nation where a part of the population is working at third world wage rates though living in a first world country. We must integrate and upgrade the "under-class" that is becoming endemic among us. It is hard to fully appreciate how rapidly globilization is generating a world economy. No amount of nationally based impediments will stand in the way of an ultimate world market economy where those nations producing most economically and efficiently will dominate world markets and generate jobs and prosperity for their citizens. The winners will not be those exploiting ignorance and low pay, but those generating a highly trained work force that will benefit from high productivity.

No nation is more favorably positioned to enter that competition than the U.S. but we cannot rely on the superiority of the past to assure future preeminence. It was an enormous strategically strong move when the United States recognized the need for universal free public education. It is absolutely necessary that we now realize that free education through high school, for the benefit of society, is now insufficient. We need to extend that another four years and so structure it so that highly qualified technical workers as well as knowledgeable concerned world citizens come out of that program. Those qualified would go on from there for professional training, advanced study and research. Such an investment would also be a huge economic stimulus.

Recognizing the need for a massive investment in education of our entire citizenry, both young and old, to their responsibilities as world citizens, their knowledge, understanding and acceptance of other cultures, the ability to communicate with a world community, and to compete favorably with workers anywhere is the single most important issue of our time. If we fail to recognize and act on that we will deserve our destiny.

# Good Wishes To The Union Of South Africa

5-5-94

All the world is watching and wondering if so divided and divisive a situation as has existed in South Africa can be brought together into the freedom and security of a law-abiding democracy. Nelson Mandela appears to be elected as the president. He has made reconciliation his main goal. He has the world's good wishes.

The obstacles to success are gargantuan. To reach everyone with education is one. To build an infrastructure of water supply, sewer systems, health facilities, jobs and incomes of decent level is another. Great expectations can also be a problem.

On the substantial plus side are the rich resources of land, forests, mineral deposits and established businesses. If Mandela can get people to turn away from their differences and concentrate on building a working democracy of the people, by the people and for the people it can be done. It will be little short of a miracle.

There undoubtedly will be severe bumps along the way. It is to be hoped the good wishes that all extend to the new administration will be supplemented with generous help and investment.

⚜ ⚜ ⚜ ⚜

## Seeking A Stable Realistic Role In World Affairs

### 8-18-94

Our recent national efforts in world affairs have done little to improve our own international situation, add to our stature in world affairs, or had much effect in the areas where we have participated or led intervention and activity. It is hard to avoid the conclusion that our efforts have been more designed to create the public perception of international leadership and strength without undertaking the serious long range commitments that many situations require.

There is a certain arrogance in feeling that we are the only ones who care and must respond. It is time for a clearer realization that we cannot solve the whole world's problems. Other nations may have a truer idea of the scope of undertakings and a truer and franker realization of their own limitations and thus, regretfully, do not take on every unfortunate situation that develops.

In more than one case we have expended resources, risked and sacrificed lives, then withdrawn, with little or no long range gain to show for our efforts. We have sought United Nations Security Council approval for nearly unilateral action without a careful study and commitment to the long range need. Sometimes we have bluffed ultimatums, only to have them called, to our embarrassment.

There would be a great advantage in getting grass roots expression of just what role American citizens would like the nation to play, how to play it, and what resources to bring to bear—having in mind the state of our own national finances and the many domestic problems needing attention.

Conferences could be initiated in counties, moved to congressional districts, then to state meetings and finally a National Conference on America's Role in World Affairs. Something must be done. We need a national course that is stable, predictable and long range, with full consideration of our own national self interest, and realistic appraisal of our current capabilities. We emerged as the victor in the cold war. Concurrently, democracy was on the increase throughout the world. Our nation had the best opportunity in this century to exert a shared world leadership for our own and the common good. We have failed to grasp that opportunity. It is time we developed a strategy and insisted on bipartisan implementation.

🌲🌳🌳🌲

## *Putting Cyberspace Communication In Perspective*

### 8-3-95

Excitement over cyberspace communication, E-mail, and other potentials generates reminiscence of the lively interest that attended the development of radio.

Guglielmo Marconi, born in Bologna, Italy in 1874, was the father of radio. From research with electromagnetic fields and transmitting for longer distances he caused a sensation when he broadcast across the English channel and a world event when he sent wireless signals across the Atlantic Ocean in 1901. Development was rapid, military applications were found for use in World War 1. By the end of the war voice radio was being broadcast by several U. S. and foreign stations and the public was caught up in a new craze.

Whether with a little squawking crystal set and head phones or more elaborate apparatus that had a speaker, listeners would stay glued to the set for hours. Neighbors would gather at the home with the first set. It became popular to keep a log of stations—the more distant the better. WGN Chicago was a favorite, so was KDKA Pittsburgh. The Kansas City Nighthawks were a favorite with the night owls.

Quickly stations joined to form networks and stations like WCCO came into being to bring network programs such as Burns and Allen, the story of Helen Trent and many others as well as frequent news broadcasters. From searching the skies for programs throughout the world radio became and continues a very local service.

All this comes to mind as cyberspace adventurers spend hours making contact with people and groups in distant places and join in worldwide spirited exchange. Just as some continued a keen interest in radio and even set-up two-way radio communication, some will become permanent devotees of cyberspace communication, but gradually this newest form of communication will make a continuing contribution and take its place in the total complex with most people depending on local sources.

Every communication development was expected to render others obsolete but all have survived, and at a greater pace than ever.

## Which Are Our Most Important Inventions?
### 4-15-93

It has been said that there were three early inventions which changed world history. The invention of the compass stimulated voyages of discovery, invention of printing from movable type fueled the Renaissance and the invention of gunpowder ended the feudal system.

It would make for stimulating dinner conversation to name the most important inventions or developments of our age and then determine order of importance. There have been several that quickly come to mind. Certainly the invention of radio and television have had enormous impact. The release of atomic energy has been significant and will reach full impact if economically feasible and clean atomic fusion can be achieved. Life is changing at a rapid pace with the introduction of computer technology.

Medical researchers have contributed many, maybe those in the field of geriatrics have had the greatest impact—adding 30 years to life expectancy in this century. Biological research with gene splicing has enormous possibilities only beginning to achieve potential. We should not forget the light bulb, the telephone, the automobile, the airplane, refrigeration, all of which can be credited to this age. What about space travel? We would tend to think it would not rate high yet, but what if an inhabited planet were encountered?

We would enjoy receiving letters of the results of your own thinking and conversations, with permission to publish. Which would you name the top three?

If we were to name the three developments, as opposed to inventions, with the greatest impact in our own country, we come up with three negatives. The decline of religious faith and church participation, the decline of the family as an institution, and the decline of personal morality, honesty and ethical standards. Are we too pessimistic? Three positives that could be mentioned are progress in the field of civil rights, a recognition and concern for the environment in which we live, and organization of the United Nations.

As we come toward the end of a century it might be well to ask ourselves what we have accomplished, what have we given to the future, and where are we in the total scheme of things, against standards we would hold as important. We hope you will share your thoughts with us and our readers.

*Reflections*

# What Impresses You Most About The United States?

### 3- 4-93

A young man, a displaced person from Europe, who had not been in the United States very long was asked that question during a coffee break at his place of employment. He thought for a moment and then replied: "This may surprise you, but I believe what impresses me most about the United States is the American grocery store."

"I am sure it is hard for you to imagine," he went on, "what it means to someone who never had it before, to go into a store where there is abundance, variety, wholesome quality, and purchase limited only by your means. I look around in awe every time I enter a supermarket—I can hardly believe my eyes. I am so thankful to be here."

His fellow workers were quiet and thoughtful. Each was probably thinking how much they took food supply in the United States for granted. We are tremendously well served by the many faceted food industry—the producers, on the farms, ranches, produce and fruit producing units who do the front line job of generating the basic supply. Then the processors who generate the quantities we consume, in the form we prefer, and of the quality we expect. Researchers are constantly working to develop new and better varieties, new techniques of preparation and preservation, such as freezing not so long ago, packaging in improved and more convenient ways,

Government agencies and workers play a role in establishing quality standards and processes, more informative labeling, inspection services and producer support. The transportation industry plays a vital role in moving food products from distant places of the world to be available fresh at the local store. Government and private agencies, and the generosity of many people, fill food shelves for those without sufficient resources to buy all they need.

Wholesalers and distributors do an incredible job of logistics to bring together the quantities that are needed and deliver them to the points of demand and with a minimum of waste and spoilage. Then there are the retailers who coordinate the desires of diverse customers with knowledge of the availabilities of new and fascinating products and have what people want when they want it, and in adequate quantities.

Finally, Americans spend less of their work time earning the money to pay for their food than any other people on earth. Food is a bargain when you stop to consider all the effort and investment, all the dedication of thousands upon thousands of people, so we can walk down the aisles and choose from the infinite variety of fine food that is available to us. There are a great many blessings the way of life in the United States has brought to its people but surely it is true that a modern grocery store is one of the most impressive.

🌲🌲🌲🌲

# Which Is The World's Most Popular Song?

7-1-93

We had an interesting dinner party exchange the other night asking people to guess which was the world's most popular song. One thought it must be Chinese because "that's where the most people are," another came up with "Take me out to the ball game" and it went on. When the secret was revealed which no one guessed, it was obvious and no one challenged the conclusion.

The most popular song in the world is "Happy Birthday to You." It is sung all over the world countless times every day. The tune was composed by Mildred J. Hill, a Louisville, Kentucky school teacher. Her younger sister, Patty Smith Hill was author of the lyrics which were first published in 1893 as "Good Morning to All" in a Sunday School song book. Lyrics were amended in 1924 to include the Happy Birthday stanza which became everyone's favorite birthday song.

As is so often the case, the original author and composer received little for this most popular contribution but a later copyright owner made as much as a million dollars a year from the sale of publication and reproduction rights. Mildred Hill died in 1916 without ever knowing her song was to become such a universal favorite. The copyright will expire in 2000 and then the song will enter the public domain.

When you claim something is the most or biggest in the entire world there are almost sure to be skeptics but in this case there is immediate agreement. Not only every day but probably every minute of every day people somewhere are joining in happy chorus in our world's most popular song.

# A Salute To The Community Volunteer

7–8–93

Throughout our state during these summer months, and everywhere else in the country, there are festivals, celebrations, parades, observances, pageants—every kind of community event preserving and extending local history and culture. In every case there are community volunteers, those dedicated, generous, unsung heroes and heroines of every event, who make it all happen. For every instance of people messing up their lives and communities that we read about, there are scores upon scores of community volunteers providing positive experiences for the people of our state. They are the true heartbeat of our country that far out weigh in numbers, activities, values and contributions the negatives we hear about.

It is not only during the summer, and it is not just in community events, but everywhere we turn, in churches, veterans organizations, civic and service clubs, youth groups, senior citizen service organizations they are to be found, faithfully and pridefully serving others for the joy of serving. It is a magnificent trait of our society, found in America to a greater degree than in any other nation on earth. If volunteers suddenly vanished from our scene there would be an immediate collapse of the functions of almost all organizations serving our society. Even governmental departments have important segments of volunteer activity.

There is no way to give adequate recognition to all who serve, although many organizations try. We hope that in this way we can add a word of thanks, praise and admiration for the community volunteer. Some may wonder, at times, if what they do is worth all the sacrifice and effort. It can safely be said that the work of community volunteers is the mortar that binds together the many diverse elements of our society and makes it work as well as it does for the benefit of the vast majority of our citizens. We should be aware of our shortcomings and seek to overcome them. We should, however, never forget or minimize how great this country of ours really is. One of its worthiest elements is the community volunteer.

♦♠♣♠♦

# Beware Of People With A Messianic Complex
## 7-29-93

A messianic complex is a conviction by an individual, group or organization that he, she or it is possessed of divine revelation and in carrying out its purpose he, she or it is carrying out the will of God. Such people or organizations are difficult to reason with because they believe their purpose is a divine directive, not to be questioned or compromised. Convictions can become so deeply held that any acts can be justified in fulfilling the "divine purpose." Those who stand in the way can be dealt with harshly and even put to death.

Messianic complexes are not a modern phenomenon. Lucretius, writing in the first century B.C. decried a religious judgment that took the life of a young woman. In the Pre-Columbian cultures sacrifice of human beings was practiced. Muslims gave people taken captive the choice of conversion to Islam or death. There were the Crusades and the Inquisition. People have long been persecuted for their failure to believe what the dominant authority held to be the absolute truth.

In our own country today there is a group intent on making the United States a "Christian nation." One only can wonder what would happen to non-Christians if that group were to prevail. It is a betrayal of our most fundamental principles if we permit religious intolerance to gain any foothold.

Our country was based on the basic rights of individuals including the freedom to worship as they choose. The government was specifically prohibited from fostering any religion. In the diversity that is now characteristic of our country it is important to cultivate adherence to religious freedom and respect and tolerance for different beliefs.

The ancient legend of the blind men and the elephant is so applicable here. You remember, the blind men were placed by the elephant, one holding a leg, another feeling the side, another touching an ear, still another holding the tail and each then describing an elephant. They had a great argument. Each had truth, but only part of it, and had they shared and respected each other's experience, they might have come closer to the total truth. Insistence that one has truth, the only truth and the whole truth is fanaticism and has no place in the free, searching-for-truth atmosphere of America.

🌲🌲🌲🌲

## Learning To Live Together

### 3-31-94

When people of a country are of one nationality, one language and a common culture it is easier for them to live together in peace and understanding. But even there differences can develop and varying degrees of confrontation occur. In the United States, with our enormous diversity, problems are multiplied.

We are fortunate to live in a country where diversity existed from the beginning, and laws and traditions were established to protect individual freedom. We have a history of effort and struggle to improve the freedom and opportunity of everyone. There are certain fundamentals we should regularly review and reaffirm. Here is the preamble to the Constitution of the United States:

*"We, the people of the United States, in order to form a more perfect union, establish justice, insure domestic tranquillity, provide for the common defense, promote the general welfare, and secure the blessings of liberty to ourselves and our posterity, do ordain and establish the Constitution of the United States of America."*

It is interesting to note the word 'ordain' as well as 'establish.' Ordain is an ecclesiastical word that undoubtedly was intended to give an aura of sacredness to the document as something not lightly to be changed, Despite the work that had gone into its drafting several amendments had to be adopted before the people of the states were willing to ratify it. The First Amendment has been a bulwark protecting individual rights. It reads: *"Congress shall make no law respecting an establishment of religion, or prohibiting the free exercise thereof, or abridging the freedom of speech, or freedom of the press, the right of the people peaceably to assemble, or to petition the government for a redress of grievances."*

Christians are about to celebrate Easter, one of the most joyful and hope instilling experiences of the church year. Members of the Jewish community attribute no divinity to Christ, and many Afro-Americans are drawn to Islam with a tradition different from each of the other two. One could go through literally dozens of religious beliefs held by portions of our population. Religious freedom is a special right to cherish, but it behooves everyone to respect that right in others. Much conflict in the world today relates to religious differences. Religious intolerance and racial discrimination is still apparent in our own country. As individuals we must do everything we can to resist discrimination of any kind.

🌲🌲🌲🌲

## There's A Lot To Like About America
### 6-30-94

We are an incredibly fortunate people and July 4, 1994 is a good time to shed negativism and concentrate on the marvelous accomplishments of our country and its people. This is not to blind ourselves to shortcomings. With pride in the achievements of the past we can turn to the challenges of the present with confidence and vigor. The solutions are within our capability and depend more on attitudes of people than initiatives of government.

The founding fundamental principle of individual freedom released a tremendous surge of personal creative and productive potential to generate benefits and comforts for a very high percentage of our people. Homes, plumbing, heating and cooling, clean water, electricity, radio, television, highways, cars, airplanes, abundant food, hospitals and health care, education, parks, athletic opportunities, outdoor recreation, and leisure time for release and enjoyment.

Freedom of thought, speech and religion fostered academic, literary, scientific, artistic and musical accomplishments of a high order. Any infringement of personal freedoms strikes at the heart of America. An efficient and dedicated military has protected us from invasion. Concentration of wealth, attacked so freely, has made possible much of the nation's economic base and generated voluntary giving, privately and through foundations, that is the envy of many nations. The gap, however, between the richest and poorest among us is a pressing current problem. Those most favored should not oppose efforts to equalize.

Central to our success has been an organization of government that keeps the power in the people and provides for a balance of legislative, judicial and executive authority to keep any from getting out of hand for too long. We must admit that our system is not serving all people equally well. Some are less equipped to function in a highly competitive, demanding and fast moving society. Maybe we have become self indulgent and taken for granted the benefits and neglected the individual responsibility for personal participation and contribution that a successful democracy needs from everyone.

At the beginning there was the inconsistency of declaring all people equal, but not extending that principle to people of color. Enormous strides have been made but the task is not complete. The genius of America was in its concept of individual freedom and opportunity and of limitations on government through balance of powers. If we consider where we started and how much has been accomplished, our record is one of enormous success. Let's recognize it, celebrate it, appreciate it and dedicate ourselves to doing something to make it more accessible to those who have been left behind. Those who fail, or for whom we have failed, must be aided to self esteem and accomplishment, not shoved farther into the darkness. The benefits of our society are not secure for any of us, until available to all of us.

# If Not Now, When? If Not Here, Where?

### 4-6-95

If there is one feeling that can be shared by most Americans it is enormous gratitude to be living today and in the United States of America. That is not to be smug and unappreciative of the values of life in many parts of the world, or during some of the great periods of history. It is to be factual. However, for most people, the personal freedom, the economic opportunities, the opportunity to learn and enjoy the accumulation of knowledge over the centuries, to have the benefit of medical developments, to have the incredible amenities of technological development in every area of human activity, to have the means of travel and communication, has never been equaled anywhere at anytime. For those in a position to make the most of all this one can ask if not now, when would anyone rather have lived, and if not here, where is there a preferable situation?

It is made more remarkable because human traits have not changed that much through the centuries. The earliest writings reveal men and women as very much the same as today. There was love, hate, kindness, cruelty, jealousy, talent, mental and physical disabilities, selfishness, greed, generosity—the whole range of human strength and weakness, of sensitivity and brutality. In our United States, men and women drew from the experiences and noblest ideas of the past to form a constitutional representative government and nurture a culture that has survived longer and had greater success than any other similar effort in human history.

It has a major flaw. It does not work equally well for everyone. It requires a high degree of self reliance, initiative, hard work, stability, perseverance to achieve the greatest personal success. Sometimes it seems that less attractive traits such as bullying, greed, selfishness, even dishonesty and corruption are unfairly effective and go uncorrected. Sometimes it also seems that leaders in political, media, legal, religious and other fields appeal to the lowest common denominator of human quality, understanding and attainment in their struggle for power and influence.

Springtime is nature's renewal of life, it is also another occasion for religious observances. It is a time of hope and confidence—of love and the aspiration of looking and living beyond oneself, in reaching out with compassion and forgiveness and efforts to uplift and make the best of life come true for others as well as for ourselves. Dare we hope that future generations will look back on us and say, that was a wonderful time, and they brought everyone along.

🌲🌲🌲🌲

## Traits Of A Serious American Citizen
### 11-9-95

There is no more complimentary title for a European businessman than for someone to refer to him as a "serious businessman." It means he pays attention to his affairs, he is informed, he studies, he thinks, he works. Restrained in his conversation and style, pleasant and polite but not aggressive, he has a quiet confidence that generates belief and trust.

America needs more citizens who would generate the observation, he, or she, is a serious American citizen. What would that mean? What would it signify? It would mean a citizen who was attentive to the governmental process as absolutely essential in a democracy. It would be one who knew his or her heritage through a broad based education and continuous study. It would be a person who could converse clearly and disagree civilly. It would be someone who loved America's diversity and was interested in and cared about other people and wanted happy lives for them.

It would be a person who knows and appreciates the incredible blessings of freedom, equality, opportunity, and justice that are possible in a well operating democracy. This means participating in elections, being active in the party of his or her choice and believing that any individual can make a difference and have influence in the choosing of candidates and the determination of a party platform. A serious citizen would know something about public finance, the need to pay for what we enjoy and to divide that burden fairly.

A serious American citizen would not be misled by hate mongers, by people or publications appealing to selfishness and greed, or offering programs that the citizen could sense were not in the long range best interest of the nation or the world community. To be a serious American citizen would require time, attention and commitment. But it goes with being a part of a powerful nation, of seeking peace and prosperity for all people everywhere. It is a mission. It cannot be imposed. It must be spontaneous and self generated. In a time when our wonderful country is plagued with many problems our greatest need is for individual decisions to so live that people would say "Now there's a serious American citizen."

*LaVerendrye Provincial Park in Ontario, adjacent to parts of Voyageurs National Park and the Boundary Waters Canoe Area, brings closer the realization of the dream of Ernest Oberholtzer, Sigurd Olson and many others to create an international park and wilderness recreation area stretching along the Canadian-American border from Grand Portage to Rainy Lake on the American side.*

# A New Park To Our North

### 10-23-86

LaVerendrye Provincial Park (pronounced LAV-er-en-dree) is a new park of the province of Ontario, Canada along the Minnesota-Ontario border stretching from the edge of Quetico Provincial Park at Saganaga Lake east to Middle Falls Provincial Park on the Pigeon River near Lake Superior.

The park, a waterway somewhat similar to the U.S. Wild and Scenic River classification, protects the historic water route of Pierre de LaVerendrye into the interior of Canada to develop the fur trade.

Logging is prohibited and there are designated campsites. Four development zones are provided and motorboats are permitted in some areas. Coordination with U.S. regulations, or ours with theirs will be necessary to avoid confusion but on the whole it is a splendid addition to the group of provincial parks in place and gradually extends protection over the famous voyageurs route that our national park includes.

It has been the dream of many for a long time that someday the entire distance from Grand Portage to International Falls will be one vast international park, extending well into Canada and the

United States and including recreation areas as well as the present wilderness and park designations. If time does not run out by permitting private ownership and development of key areas there is the possibility of one of the truly superlative parks of the entire world. People in Canada have been quietly working through the extension of the provincial park system. Someday it may all come together.

🌲🌳🌳🌲

# When Gold Mining Comes
### 10-27-88

It is no longer a question of whether gold will be discovered in Minnesota or if gold mining will come to our state. Gold has been discovered and it is now just a matter of when mining will begin. The trigger will be the price of gold. Experts say that when the price stabilizes at $500 an ounce gold mining in Minnesota will be economically feasible and will begin.

If an announcement of an application for a gold mining plant were made this week it would be hailed with jubilation in northeastern Minnesota where economic development and jobs are sorely needed. There would be an attitude of doing everything possible to encourage the new enterprise and any cautions or shows of resistance would be brushed aside.

Actually, gold mining, as other forms of mineral processing, can be dirty and polluting. As we have done before we urge again that our legislature check with the Department of Natural Resources and have experts on minerals review our laws relating to mining to see if they adequately protect the environment for a proposal of gold mining. Gold deposits are close to the Boundary Waters Canoe Area and the Voyageurs National Park, important resources for the state and features important to protect.

Purpose of the study would be to be ready with sound progressive statutes so that new mining developments can be encouraged but in a framework of due regard for other assets of the state and the general health and well being of our people.

## Avoiding An Environmental Shootout

7-6-95

In a significant and controversial divided decision the U.S. Supreme Court has held that government laws, rules and regulations affecting the use of private property are constitutional. The decision was on appeal of timber interests in the West on the case popularly identified as the spotted owl case. Pressure will now grow to make drastic changes in the environmental protection laws now in effect. It is important that balanced judgment and common sense prevail in seeking a working compromise.

Both sides should avoid over simplification and demeaning of each others position. On the one side there are genuine economic and job concerns needing the most serious consideration, not just "selfish, greedy, special interests who care nothing about the environment." On the other side there is a great deal more involved than "stupid bird watchers putting the welfare of spotted owls ahead of jobs and income for human beings." On both sides is the common concern for the preservation of ecological systems that will permit life on earth to continue indefinitely.

In 1962, Rachel Carson, after achieving national note as a biologist in the federal Fish and Wild Life Service and as author of *Under The Sea Wind* and *The Sea Around Us*, shocked the nation to attention with *Silent Spring*. It documented the lethal and lasting impact of pesticides as then produced and sold. It triggered the intense concern with pollution of all kinds and the long term effect on the survival of life on planet earth. Legislatures and the Congress responded to the popular demand with extensive laws and regulations pertaining to the environment, ecological systems, endangered species of plants and wildlife, and controls of many kinds on toxic emissions and wastes.

It is not impossible that some regulations went too far too fast. Maybe laws should establish standards instead of being so specific as to how to achieve them. Some compromise may be necessary and wise but there is no denying the seriousness of the situation and its global implication. At one point Rachel Carson said: "I think we are challenged as mankind has never been challenged before to prove our maturity and our mastery, not of nature, but of ourselves."

# Ice Fishing In Minnesota

### 12-28-95

Colonies of fish houses are suddenly appearing on Minnesota lakes everywhere. People in southern parts of our country think ice fishing is a form of insanity, and in other countries, particularly around the equator, they find it impossible to believe. Like many traditions, it is hard to understand until you get into it. Fishing under any conditions is a joyful addiction that ranges from sweet silence and solitude to life bonding, warm (even in a fish house) and convivial fellowship. Ice fishing has come a long way from chopping a hole in the ice and sitting on a bucket in sub-zero weather. Fish houses on Mille Lacs Lake, for example, became something of a problem by doubling as summer cabins. A modern fish house will have a power driven auger for establishing the fishing hole. It will have battery driven TV or radio or both, a chemical toilet, a propane space heater, even carpeting on the floor or over the ice. Some are even tall enough to become "two story" with bunks above for the all night enthusiasts. When it is bright outside and dark in the fish house the light will come through the hole in the ice and give the person fishing a unique view into the lake and a chance to watch the fish moving around, or perchance a turtle or other lake inhabitant. Ice fishing has its own mystique and kinship with nature that can capture a lifetime of interest. Ice fishing has its own paraphernalia and it can vary widely. There are depth sounders and radar devices that identify activity beyond sight. There are also tip-ups that are nearly robot fishermen if the card game is becoming more exciting than the fishing. There are no fish quite as fresh as those caught ice fishing. They freeze quickly and are kept perfectly until the fish crew is home. There are many outdoor joys and memorable experiences that go with life in Minnesota and ice fishing is one of them—and the colonies get a little larger each year. Fish houses tend to cluster and it takes an adventurer to strike out on his or her own. It doesn't take long for word of success to get around and soon the lone adventurer has company.

*⋆🌲🌲⋆*

*The establishment of Voyageurs National Park in 1971 was spearheaded by the author in 1962 during his term as governor when he invited Conrad Wirth, director of the National Park Service and a native Minnesotan, to tour the area of the proposed park. This visit began a successful 9-year effort to secure a national park for Minnesota.*

## National Park Celebration

8-22-91

Minnesota has a double national park celebration coming up next Sunday, the 25th. This year is the 75th anniversary of the National Park Service and the 20th milestone of the Congressional act that authorized Minnesota's Voyageurs National Park, just east of International Falls.

America's first national park and the first national park in the world, Yellowstone, was established in 1872. It was a long time before we had a National Park Service. Administration of the parks was first in the hands of the Interior Department. When a prominent and wealthy park visitor wrote a letter of complaint, he was invited to come to Washington and run them. Stephen Tye Mather had written "Scenery is a hollow enjoyment to a tourist who sets out after an indigestible breakfast and fitful sleep on an impossible bed." In response to Secretary Franklin Lane's challenge, Mather said he would come if Horace Albright, a young Washington land and mining lawyer would join him. The pairing was arrranged and the National Park Service established on August 25th, 1916. It has become one of the most respected of the national agencies. It is currently beset with tough financial and maintenance problems as park use expands far faster than the means to cope with the increased use.

In Minnesota efforts to win national park status go back as far as 1891 when a legislative resolution memorialized Congress to establish a national park here. That and several subsequent efforts came to nothing until a group of state, national and private business representatives toured the Kabetogema area in June of 1962 and agreed the area was worthy of study for a national park. It took nine years to complete the planning and obtain the necessary federal legislation which was signed by President Nixon in January of 1971. But this was the authorization only and it took four more years to accomplish the land acquisitions and consolidations to justify "establishing" the park which occurred in 1975. Then there were years of obtaining funds to provide the visitors center and other facilities to fully accommodate visitors. That took until 1987. Now the park is in wonderful condition to use, by those bringing their own equipment, or by tourists without equipment enjoying a boat ride, hike, canoe trip all made available with equipment and facilities.

Minnesotans can be proud of Voyageurs National Park but it, like all the others, takes constant vigilance to protect its precious values for all time, and to see that sufficient funds are available for adequate maintenance and staffing. A program is scheduled, starting at 12 noon Sunday at the Rainy Lake visitors center, to mark the anniversary.

🌲🌳🌳🌲

*This State park, in the heart of the Twin Cities area, was called the metro region's "Central Park" by the late Judge C. R. Magney. It was one of several new state parks created during the governorship of the author.*

## Discover Fort Snelling State Park
### 9-19-96

Last Thursday noon a happy company of people met in Ft. Snelling State Park to break ground for the Thomas C. Savage Visitor Center. It was at a beautiful rise overlooking the Minnesota River a short distance from its confluence with the Mississippi. It was the culmination of eight years of concentrated effort, marked by a number of delays and disappointments. It was also 35 years after the Legislature established the park. For many years the land below Ft. Snelling was overlooked and ignored. Tom Savage, St. Paul businessman and member of a pioneer Minnesota family who spent his life working on park and environmental projects, was one of the first of those who early felt the large area, despite danger of periodic flooding, was a pristine natural area in the heart of a metropolitan area with wonderful park possibilities. Ft. Snelling had been turned over to the state and Gov. Orville Freeman directed the Department of Transportation to put Highway 494 under Fort Snelling rather than cutting through it. The Legislature responded with generous restoration appropriations and two fine facilities resulted—the restored fort now under the direction of the Minnesota Historical Society and the park administered by the Department of Natural Resources.

The parks division of the DNR has done a fine job of development with auto access, bike and hiking trails, and preservation of the sense of wildness one feels when in the park. The entry is off the Post Road which leaves 494 close to the airport. There is a splendid cover of trees and undergrowth and the area is a haven for water and land birds as well as small animal life. One feels a sense of history with the two rivers coming together at the spot where young visionary Col. Josiah Snelling thought a fort should be built. He did such a superlative job the War Department decided to name it for him.

Those who come to know the Ft. Snelling State Park area love it, as did American Indians for hundreds of years, but it is still relatively undiscovered by the greater part of the metro population. Even a few minutes drive around it is refreshing. Few cities of the country have such a marvelous natural area so conveniently close.

# Liberty Enlightening the World

7-3-86

It all started at a dinner party in a country home near Versailles in 1865. Edouard Rene Lefebvre de Leboulaye was the host for a group of friends, who, like him, abhorred the dictatorial regime of Louis Napoleon Bonaparte (Napoleon III) established by force in 1851 and still maintained. How could the French people be shown there was a better form of government and won over to a peaceful revolution? This was the after dinner discussion as it had been many times before. The enlightened dinner guests were as much opposed to a bloody revolution as they were to Bonaparte.

Across the ocean was the appealing example of the United States of America with a republican form of government through which the people had found the way to provide order and liberty—freedom under law, with restraints on the central power, protecting the rights of the individual.

At one point Laboulaye wondered aloud what the result might be if France or the French people were to present a colossal statue dedicated to liberty to the young successful republic. Would it focus the attention of the French on the advantages of a free society and generate desire for change?

A young sculptor, Frederic Auguste Bartholdi, who had a penchant for colossal statues was present and responded enthusiastically to the idea as did the others. Opportunity for action came when Bonaparte and France suffered a crushing defeat by Prussia in 1870. Bonaparte was deposed and the republican forces seized the opportunity to establish a constitutional state, the Third Republic. Now was the time to dramatize the issue and what better way than proposing to give a statue of "Liberty Enlightening the

World" to that nation where the new French idealism had its reality and whose freedom the French had helped secure.

Bartholdi was dispatched to the United States in 1871. He was immediately captivated by the site of Bedloe's Island and all he talked to responded favorably to the idea. The French public was thrilled and plans proceeded. Bartholdi was to design the statue with the engineering help of Gustave Eiffel and in America Richard Norris Hunt was to produce the base with funds raised here. There was enthusiasm but contributions lagged until Joseph Pulitzer, journalist and publisher, gave leadership to raising the final $100,000.

In 1883 at one of the U.S. fund raising events F. Hopkinson Smith read a poem by a young author, Emma Lazarus, written in honor of the project. It was well received but given no further notice for 20 years. Meanwhile she died. A friend remembered the stirring words of the writing and in 1903 obtained permission to place a plaque at the entrance to the statue with the lines of "The New Colossus" which conclude:

> *"Give me your tired, your poor,*
> *Your huddled masses yearning to breathe free,*
> *The wretched refuse of your teeming shore,*
> *Send these, the homeless, tempest-tossed to me,*
> *I lift the lamp beside the golden door."*

A few years ago the idea was generated that the Statue of Liberty should be refurbished to mark the 100th anniversary of the dedication and celebrate that anniversary on July 4th 1986. We don't know but maybe the idea had its origin at a dinner party of some liberty loving patriots who thought this would be a subtle and effective way to remind Americans of the ideals that are basic to our system of government.

The idea caught on, more than $200 million was raised, the

work has been accomplished and a new unveiling takes place this week amid several days of celebration like nothing since the bicentennial in 1976.

Despite failures and shortcomings there is an incredible record of accomplishment by our people in the 100 years and this week is the time to honor that record and feel gratitude for the opportunities that have come to each of us as a result. With a foot raised for a further step and the torch held high to light the way, the statue suggests the continuing development of liberty. The woman with the torch is a magnificent symbol of this ideal. No one ever forgets the first sight of the statue and particularly the first view of that figure facing out to sea as one returns from a stay abroad. It is a reminder and encouragement of how deep-seated is the yearning in all of us for universal recognition of that noble conviction that "all men are created equal and are endowed, by their Creator, with certain unalienable rights, and that among these are life, liberty and the pursuit of happiness."

# How Lucky We Are
## To Be Alive—Today—In America!

10-28-94

Recently I read of the birth of pre-mature twins. They were tiny and at high risk of survival. All the skill of modern medical technology was directed at their survival. At first it was just that and barely successful. Then the tide turned and the little bodies converted nourishment into tissue and muscle and they began to grow. They are now safely on their way to good health, The attending physicians said that had those two little tots been born a year earlier they would not have made it—the technology would not have been adequate.

We live at a time of enormous technical progress in every possible field and enjoy the benefits of generations of progress. If we were to suddenly be without all that has been added to our lives in the last 100 years, we would be slowed down to a walk or a horse's trot, would be depending on candlelight, and if we wanted to talk to relatives or friends we would have to go where they were. We would work from dawn to dusk to provide for our basic needs.

Think then of 500 years ago when printing from movable type was developed and the first books were published, or 1000, 2000, 5000 years ago. We don't know how it is that we happened to be born in this time of history and into the families and lands where we find ourselves. It is a profound mystery. But here we are, the beneficiaries of all that has gone before.

What are the results of living now in America instead of at some earlier time? We certainly live longer as a result of medication, surgery, sanitation, nutritious food, and all other changes affecting health. In the last century alone, 30 years have been added to life expectancy. We live better, travel easier to anywhere in the world, communicate better and are kept better informed. There is little in common with life today and even 100 years ago.

One of the most dramatic changes has been in the use of time. As earlier mentioned early days in America meant constant work for survival. Today for relatively few hours a week we take care of our basic needs and make provision for the future. I have seen substantial change in hours of work in my own lifetime. As a boy I worked 54 hours a week, 7 to 12, 12:20 to 5:20 five days a week and

8 to 12 on Saturday. We have more "disposable time now." Small children in the family can surely use up that disposable time, particularly for women combining home making and work outside the home. But for society as a whole there is time for optional pursuits. It will probably be one of the measures of our society, by historians—what we did with our disposable time—did we pursue education, travel, service to others or did we use it all for pleasure and self indulgence. Most families budget and plan expenses against income; how well do we budget and use our free time?

Just think what it means to live in a democracy and to have the protection of a court system. Life is not perfect but it is well to occasionally stop and review the situation to bring home to us how lucky we are to be living—today—and in America.